D0262835

living together

living together

edited by David Kennard & Neil Small
with a foreword by Robin Skynner

Quartet Books

First published in Great Britain in 1997 by
Quartet Books Limited
A member of the Namara Group
27 Goodge Street
London W1P 2LD

A catalogue record for this title is available from the British Library

ISBN 0 7043 8020 X

Phototypeset by The Harrington Consultancy, London
Printed and bound in Finland by WSOY

Contents

FOREWORD

Those of a reflective nature, in this *fin de siècle* period, will almost be preoccupied by questions such as how will the world change in the next century? What do I need to now prepare for these changes?

The most useful article I have found on this subject was very short – two sides of one sheet of paper. It came from the United States, though I do not know how or who sent it – it may have fallen out of the Family Therapy Network or come in the same envelope. The gist of this article was that at the moment we were at an extraordinary pause, like a comma in a sentence. We cannot finish the sentence, nor can we start the next sentence until we have done so. The conclusion reached was that we have to wait for the next sentence to come along. We cannot force anything, we must just wait and remain open to illumination if it comes. Although we can wait alone, we can wait together, in company, and these ideas have led to the formation of groups of people in different parts of the USA, particularly California, where they can wait together.

This seems true to me; to make sense. But reflecting upon it, I realize that when I reach a comma in a sentence and do not know how to proceed, I need to read again what I have already written, and see the direction in which I was going so that I can continue on that course and bring the sentence to a conclusion. Then maybe I can start the next.

This article, entitled 'Transition 2000', said that this gathering together of groups of people to wait hopefully was not a new form of psychotherapy, not a religion, not a political movement.

Even if we cannot force the pace for the arrival of the new paradigm, we can at least reflect on what we know already, tidy it up a bit and bring it to some conclusion. This splendid book, which I have greatly enjoyed reading and found very stimulating to further thought, reflects upon the ideas developed in psychoanalytic work, and tries to apply these to form clearer ideas of issues in the social dimension – politics, economics and so on. The authors and editors are well equipped for this task.

This book shows us where we are and even takes us a bit further, providing us with a sound basis from which new political and economic ideas could spring when the time is right. I recommend it highly to all those working with groups of different sizes and also to those concerned with the development of more satisfactory political, economic and social principles.

Robin Skynner
London, 1996

INTRODUCTION

We live together in a world that is going through unprecedented changes. Families break up and regroup. Parents no longer have the certainties of what's right and what's wrong to tell their children. Almost anything goes, it seems. Employers can no longer be expected to look after their workers. The fat cats cream off quick profits while the workforce is restructured. Few, it seems, are safe from the scrap heap. The images of pleasure and success that surround us and invite us to join their make-believe world surely only make it harder for us to work at making ordinary life a success – so unexciting, complicated and frustrating by comparison. And as if all this were not enough, we have to learn to live within the limits imposed by what we now know about the earth's finite resources.

This book grew out the idea that psychotherapists and counsellors, whose work gives them a particular insight into what goes wrong in people's lives, might have some interesting things to say about all these changes and about what would make our society a better place to live in and for children to grow up in.

What we had in mind was to ask this question: *Could the knowledge and understanding gained through nearly a century of psychoanalytically informed work with individuals, families, groups and organizations be used to contribute towards a practical agenda for social change that would increase our emotional health and well-being?* We wanted to bring together the themes and ideas that emerged from this question into one readable book that would focus attention on the contribution that psychotherapists and counsellors can make – in some cases already are making – to the wider debate about the nature of our society as we approach the twenty-first century.

In offering the contributions of psychotherapists and counsellors to these issues we know we are opening ourselves to the charge of claiming some sort of superior wisdom, or of trying to undermine the independence and resolve of the individual citizen. We are not saying that if everyone had psychotherapy the world would be a better place. Nor are we claiming that psychotherapists have better answers than anyone else. Clear-cut *answers* are almost certainly not the answer to what collectively ails us. What we are saying is that psychotherapists and counsellors have a particular angle on the problems of contemporary lives, and that their views, along with those of others, can have a beneficial influence on the way these problems are addressed.

How the book began

In the spring of 1994 one of the book's editors, David Kennard, invited a number of colleagues to meet to talk about what psychotherapists and counsellors might be able to contribute to wider social problems. Two years earlier, after working for twenty-five years as a clinical psychologist and group analyst in the National Health Service, David had gone to work at The Retreat, a small psychiatric hospital in York managed by Quakers ever since it opened in 1796. The Retreat was the first mental hospital built for the then revolutionary purpose of trying to treat mental distress in a humanitarian way, through the use of personal relationships and social expectations, an approach that was known as moral treatment. At the beginning of the 1990s The Retreat wanted to rekindle its pioneering role and offered David the chance to become director of a new venture, the Tuke Centre for Psychotherapy and Counselling, named after the founder of The Retreat, William Tuke.

Like all psychotherapy and counselling services, the Tuke Centre could provide psychological help for people who recognize they need it and are able to ask for it. Providing such help is an important task, and doing it well is difficult, but the benefits are limited to those who make it to the door, and perhaps their relatives, friends and colleagues. One question this raised was that if psychotherapists and counsellors understand more than most about what goes wrong in people's lives, could this understanding be of value to people who do not seek psychotherapy but still struggle with the wider problems in our society – the sort of problems that become the subject of 'moral panics' or outrage in the media and always seem to imply a breakdown in shared values and social cohesion?

Thus was the Social Project for Psychotherapists and Counsellors born. The colleagues whom David approached became a focus group, sharing a psychoanalytic basis in their work, that decided to meet regularly to discuss how they could translate their interest into some form of practical action. Gradually the idea that a book would be a good starting point took shape. It needed to be a book that would bridge the gap between the world of professional therapists and people who would never usually read or think about psychotherapy. A popular book in the best sense. And it needed to be part of a process, something that would set balls rolling without knowing exactly where that might lead, apart from forward.

And if we were concerned with social change we needed to be able to relate the psychoanalytic view to how others, sociologists and social theorists in particular, saw what was happening to the economy, to work, to the family and to the way that individuals went about understanding the world they lived in. This was the particular viewpoint Neil Small brought to the book. After

3

studying Political Science and Social Work he worked in a therapeutic community. His time there was short but, for him, influential. He went on to work in a local authority social services department and then moved into university teaching. In recent years he had been involved in research into a number of topics connected with health and social care. Getting involved as an editor of this book renewed a long-time contact with David and connected with a continuing interest in psychoanalysis and social change.

In addition to Neil and David the members of the Social Project focus group have been James Anderson, a freelance counsellor, Joanne Blackley, a psychotherapist in private practice, Alan Dunnett, a university counsellor and counsellor trainer, Paul Keeble, director of WPF North, a counselling centre, Lesley Murphy, a freelance counsellor and trainer, and Celly Rowe, a consultant psychotherapist and psychiatrist in the National Health Service.

Building the book

To create the best book we could imagine we invited a number of key people to contribute to the project. We asked Susie Orbach, Dorothy Rowe, Andrew Samuels, Valerie Sinason and Robin Skynner, all experienced psychotherapists whom we knew had the passion and the skill to communicate their understanding of the human condition to a wide audience. We asked Bob Hinshelwood and Rob Weatherill, two psychoanalysts whose capacity to explore the links between the human mind and cultural trends we greatly admired. And we asked Eric Miller, Barry Richards and Stuart Whiteley, whose psychoanalytically informed work with (respectively) organizations, the sociology of popular culture and therapeutic communities we felt would add further depth and range to the picture we wanted to build. To give continuity to their contributions we asked each of them to take these three questions as their starting point:

1 *Through your work in the field of mental health what do you think you have learned about what it is like to live in today's society?*

2 *How do you respond to what you have learned, personally and professionally?*

3 *In the light of your answers what new arrangements/ activities/structures do you think would make our society a better place to live in?*

As the book took shape a number of things emerged. One was that we were not alone in our interest in looking at society through the window of working with individuals who experienced themselves as failing, in their sense of themselves, in their relationships or their work. In America and Britain we found groups with similar aims. One of these was Psychotherapists and Counsellors for Social Responsibility, an organization started in 1995 by a group which included some of the contributors to this book. Another thing that emerged was that our goal of creating a 'practical agenda for social change' was not going to happen, at least not in any straightforward sense. Instead our goal began to change towards something more elusive and evocative – hints and glimpses rather than practical proposals, although some of the latter remained. As the book took shape, connections also arose between different chapters. Themes began to emerge. We were excited by the sense of something growing before our eyes and we hope this excitement conveys itself to our readers.

The theme that emerged most consistently was the loss of certainty across whole tracts of our emotional and cultural lives: the structure of the family; the sources of authority that contain our intergroup tensions; our identity in relation to the workplace; the failure and fading of old economic and ideological polarities. Related to this broad theme are different future scenarios, from great optimism for new social structures and assumptions to barely glimpsed hopes for any sustainable intimacy. The optimistic message contained within the book is that this loss of certainties – in family life, work, culture, politics, economics – need not be seen as a disaster. New notions and ways of thinking are emerging that offer us possible ways forward: education for emotional literacy, new ideas about the value of popular culture, a growing awareness of the connections between our personal, political and economic selves, new forms of social collective that do not rely on a shared ideology to hold them together. On the other hand, there are serious causes for doubt and apprehension, questions we need to start to get to grips with. How adaptable is human nature? Can we rein back the self-interest that characterized the 1980s? Can we give up the belief in the possibility of a comprehensive, rational analysis of our world? What happens when we no longer have a sense that things will work out better in the end, that overall we are making progress? And what is left of our deeper selves as a welter of images and information distracts and threatens to engulf us?

In putting this book together we have acted in a way that we think is better described as hosts rather than as conventional editors. Along with the other members of our Social Project focus group we have been very involved not just with what has been contributed but in trying to see the different chapters from the point of view of our readers. We wanted to invite people in and introduce everyone to each other. Between chapters we offer commentaries which are based on the lively, sometimes heated, discussions of the Social Project group as we read each chapter, making connections with our own professional and personal experiences and looking at how the chapters connected with each other as similar issues were addressed by different contributors. We have also tried to unpack and explain some of the ideas offered where we felt this would be helpful. Doing this has stretched and educated us in ways we had not anticipated and through this we feel enriched.

This book probably would not have happened, certainly not in its present form, without our separate past experience of therapeutic communities with their daily community meetings where opposing views could be aired, explored and sometimes reconciled. The sort of living together experienced in such settings has provided a continuing image and reference point for the construction of the book. The principle on which these communities work is that the experience of living together is not the background to therapy, it *is* the therapy. Open communication and shared decision-making set a certain tone in which others gradually come to be seen as fellow-members of the human race rather than as superior critics or as opponents, and each individual comes to see himself or herself as a valued but ordinary member of the group, neither an outcast nor especially wonderful. Such lessons, and processes, filter into this book in both its style and its message.

Introducing our contributors

We asked each of our contributors to relate the three questions stated earlier to an area of particular concern to them.

Our first contributor is Stuart Whiteley, who sets the scene by describing the history of therapeutic communities and summarizes how they work. Stuart's chapter is followed by Susie Orbach writing about the family. Susie's central theme is change in what we recognize as the form the family must take, in the roles of mothers and fathers, and in our ideas about children and childhood. She argues that for relationships to be a source of inner security the family does not need to keep to any predetermined form but there does need to be a sufficient degree of emotional literacy. Valerie Sinason continues on the subject of childhood, focusing on the vulnerability of children to the effects of poverty and abuse but also on the potential for overcoming these. Using personal and research evidence she comes up with a surprisingly optimistic hypothesis. Rob Weatherill takes us in the direction of postmodernism and the collapse of all certainties. Writing with complexity and passion, Rob argues that there is little left that is solid or deep in our relationships, only surfaces and images. He suggests there may just be a chance to do something about this. Barry Richards takes a different view of the impact of popular culture: that increasingly – through sport and therapeutically aware television soaps – it may provide the emotional containment that is lacking in traditional family life and other traditional sources of authority.

Eric Miller focuses on the profound shift over the past fifteen years in the relationship between individuals and their work, which he sees as a process of psychological withdrawal as the workplace loses its capacity to provide emotional security and identity. He suggests there may be new possibilities for emotional engagement in work. Possibilities for a different basis for social engagement is a theme taken up by our final group of contributors. Bob Hinshelwood examines the genesis of ideology and its tendency to find its way into every aspect of our group relations. A willingness to be mistaken and to come together in groups based on creativity rather than ideas may offer us ways out of the ideological maze. Dorothy Rowe sounds a strong note of scepticism about the capacity of /humans in general and psychotherapists and psychologists in particular to accept that they are mistaken, especially when status and power are at stake. Finally Andrew Samuels challenges readers to stretch their thinking about the wider applications of psychotherapy with his analysis of politics and economics – to quote Schumacher – 'as if people mattered'. His analysis is that the era of ideological opposition between implacable foes is over and there is everything to play for.

Setting the scene

This is a book that confesses to, actually is built on, a number of paradoxes or contradictions. It is an 'ideas' book that mistrusts ideas; it is a book that looks towards the future while disclaiming any powers of prediction; and it is a book that, while proclaiming the loss of those certainties that used to guide us, has its roots firmly planted in the past. Those roots involve three traditions.

One tradition, which is probably as old as society, is the attempt to recognize the fellow human being in another person who may at first appear mad, bad or dangerous. This compassionate sentiment is part of many religious and humanist creeds. It was expressed by Quakers in the belief that there is 'that of God in every man', a belief that underpinned the development of moral treatment which was the first attempt to create a social environment that was psychologically therapeutic. Many of our contributors share the conviction that a central task for individuals in today's society is not to prejudge our fellow human beings and to recognize the limits of our ability to understand another's experience, especially where that person belongs to a different group, class or culture.

Another tradition, scientific, therapeutic and cultural, is psychoanalysis and the analytic therapies. Freud introduced the term psychoanalysis exactly a hundred years ago to describe a form of treatment for neurosis based on the interpretation of the patient's unconscious feelings and attitudes. Many schools of psychotherapy have evolved since then – a generally accepted estimate puts the present number at four hundred – many of them directly or indirectly taking psychoanalysis as their starting point. Countless volumes and papers have been written arguing for and against the validity and the value of psychoanalytically based therapies. This book is not intended as a contribution to that particular debate. What it is contributing to is the tradition of using the insights and concepts of psychoanalytically based work to look at and think about the human condition more widely.

The third tradition, which has grown up in the last fifty years, has been the attempt to bring these first two traditions together within a social framework: to study the relationship between the individual and his or her social environment, to understand how individuals impact on their environment and vice versa. This is the field of social psychology, social anthropology, studies of organizations and – when applied to individuals with severe emotional problems – therapeutic communities.

Although never fully accepted by the professional establishment, therapeutic communities provided (and still provide) generations of mental health workers with the experience of struggling towards real communication and openness rather than operating within the stereotypes and assumptions that so often separate those labelled as 'sick' and 'well'. The struggle to create a potential space for honest, open communication is at heart what all psychotherapy, and much of this book, are about.

To explain more about this third tradition we start the book with a look at how therapeutic communities began.

Chapter 1
MAKING A HOSPITAL THERAPEUTIC
J. Stuart Whiteley

In the early 1940s a handwritten sign appeared outside the recreation room of a military psychiatric hospital at Northfield in Birmingham. It simply read THE CLUB. To those who inquired as to the nature of the club, the officer in charge, a former mathematics teacher now serving in the Education Corps and posted to the hospital after duties on War Office selection boards, answered, 'It is whatever you like it to be' (Main, 1983).

The hospital was one of two special units set up by the War Office to respond to the large numbers of service personnel who were experiencing emotional and psychosomatic disorders in response to the stress of war experiences. At one of these units, Northfield, the staff team had been drawn largely from the Tavistock Clinic, a leading centre for psychoanalytic practice and teaching in England, and was using the then new techniques of group psychotherapy. At the other unit, at Mill Hill in north

London, the team was drawn from the more medically oriented Maudsley Hospital and was headed by Maxwell Jones.

Although the philosophies of the two units were initially different and there was little contact between them, both units came up with a similar observation: that the cause of the present disability was rooted in *social malfunctioning*. In the treatment process therefore it was important to examine social interactions, '*here and now*', in the daily routine of the artificially constructed community of the hospital. In the exploration of the common disorder it was essential to *openly communicate* all information about the disorder, to enlist each person in a *shared responsibility* for the therapeutic management of themselves and their fellows and to *remove the barriers*, such as the hierarchical authority structure of the institution, which stood in the way of freedom of expression and participation in the daily management of the unit and the individuals within it.

At Mill Hill, Maxwell Jones began by lecturing to his patients on the anatomical and physiological structure of the central nervous system. Lectures became dialogues between the 'teacher' and the 'students' and then group discussions. Topics were more about war experiences and everyday life in the hospital than symptom causation. At Northfield it was noted how disturbance in one section of the hospital could affect the morale and functioning of the whole unit and how conditions prevailing outside the hospital could effect behaviour within the hospital. When the war was going badly the patients went around in the distinctive 'hospital blues' uniform of wounded soldiers; when the war was going well they preferred to be seen in their regimental uniforms with battalion badges, as Desert Rats, etc.

Antecedents of the therapeutic community

There has been a long history of humanitarian responses to people with mental illness. During the nineteenth century there had been a number of innovative approaches which adhered to the principles of treating them not only with compassion but also as still significant human beings and members of society. Charles Dickens

11

noted in his account of his visits to the Boston State Hospital, Massachusetts, in 1842:

> Every patient in this asylum sits down to dinner every day with a knife and fork and in the midst of them sits the gentleman [the Superintendent Physician] ... at every meal moral influence alone restrains the more violent, the effect of that influence ... as a means of restraint, to say nothing of it as a means of cure, is a hundred times more efficacious than all the strait waistcoats, fetters. (Dickens, 1842)

Although such endeavours were, in the main, based on humanitarian or religious principles the therapeutic effects inherent in these hospital communities and of the impact of participation in communal activities was not lost on reformers. In England, William Tuke at The Retreat, introduced occupation for the patients, noting that: 'The immediate object is not the value of the labour but the benefit of the patient .... [and] nursing their fellow patients is a valuable occupation for both sexes ....' (Whiteley & Gordon, 1979).

This 'era of moral treatment', as it came to be called, came to an end by the close of the nineteenth century. There were two reasons for this. The first was the emerging factory system of industrial production based on large organizations, highly regimented and seeking uniformity of product. This form of social organization became a paradigm for institutions more generally and was replicated in hospitals and prisons, many of which still exist (see Foucault, 1967; Rohman, 1971). The second was the fact that the discoveries of biological researchers and psychoanalysis combined to assert that the individual on his or her own was the focus for understanding mental illness. The pendulum swung right away from all attempts at looking at the social context – of either cause or treatment. The result was a reversion to closed asylum practices. Medication and various physical treatments dominated.

The development of the therapeutic community

After the wartime experience in the military hospitals many doctors returning to civilian life sought to emulate the successful experiences at Mill Hill and Northfield. Ward meetings and discussion groups were introduced. What were not grasped were the salient points of real shared responsibility, open communication and patient participation in management. When the pharmaceutical industry began to address psychiatric disorders by producing tranquillizing and antidepressant drugs there was a quick return, in most institutions, to the medically determined therapies.

The deflection of those with the so-called more serious mental illnesses (schizophrenia, psychotic depression, etc.) towards medical and physical treatments inadvertently left behind a pool of clients whose problems were more clearly rooted in poor early life experiences made manifest by social dysfunction such as an inability to sustain work or relationships, criminal behaviour, alcohol or drug abuse. These characteristics were usually lumped together under the diagnosis of personality disorder. In a few hospitals such as the Cassel Hospital, Richmond, where Tom Main had gone after Northfield, and in Belmont (later Henderson Hospital), Sutton, where Maxwell Jones went the idea of the hospital as a therapeutic community continued to develop. This development concentrated on the further exploration and understanding of social malfunctioning, its causes, and treatment through attention to social processes. Within a functioning therapeutic community there was full opportunity to examine relationships and how they were formed, how misunderstandings arose, how everyone would be in some way affected by events within the boundaries of the community and how, by the collaboration of all members of the community, the malfunctioning could be put right.

A typical treatment programme in a therapeutic community would begin the day with a full community meeting of staff and patients (usually called 'residents' to diminish the 'illness' inference of being designated a patient). This large group forum would review events of the previous day and would allow current issues with residents to be voiced. Smaller psychotherapeutic groups would follow, directed more to dealing with intra-personal issues among the residents and finding links with both the here-and-now events in the community and past experiences outside. Then might follow work groups in which residents and staff would carry out the real-life tasks of maintaining the unit, cooking the meals, preparing social events or otherwise attending to daily affairs. The principles of shared responsibility between staff and residents, open communication, respect for another's point of view and full participation in all activities of the unit would be sustained. But the opportunities for examining how each individual interacted in the daily round, whether in 'therapy groups', 'management groups' or 'work groups', and for confrontation and suggestion as to how any adverse behaviour might be modified and new behaviour substituted would also be maintained by punctuating the round of activities with reflective discussion groups involving all immediately concerned. Interaction, exploration and experimentation would be key processes.

In the military situation, stress and breakdown occurred when individuals, previously living a relatively normal life style, with clear boundaries around themselves and with family, social, occupational, residential and other ties and expectations, were traumatically thrown into an unforeseen situation which called for resources and responses that they did not possess. The change required to cope with the new situation proved too much for them and help was required to find the necessary resources from within.

In the civilian situation the precipitating factor was usually that the individuals found themselves, similarly, in a situation with which they could not cope but this time it was rather the obverse of the above scenario. His or her prior life will have been set in a fixed mode of interaction with others which may well be regarded as abnormal. Usually, in cases of serious social malfunction, there will have been traumatic events in early life which have resulted in a defensive retreat from society and the adoption of methods of coping – such as alcoholism, drug addiction, suicide attempts or lawbreaking – in order to survive or to get back at what is seen as an unfair society. The potentially traumatic change he/she now has to face is to risk beginning to interact with society in a less defensive and more collaborative way.

Learning from the therapeutic community

The basic principles of the therapeutic-community process have already been alluded to. Research work on the practice has added to our knowledge. Robert Rapoport (1960), a social anthropologist, elicited four fundamental themes from investigations at the Henderson Hospital in the late 1950s. These were permissiveness, reality confrontation, democratization and communalism. But it was not enough just to 'install' these processes and hope for results. Further investigations of curative factors in the therapeutic community (Collis & Whiteley, 1987) showed that people coming into the Henderson community, in the initial stages, valued acceptance and the instillation of hope. Later, when they felt more secure within the community, they began to gain from self-understanding and learning from their interaction with others. Permissiveness allows for catharsis and self-disclosure and the assumption of self-responsibility. Reality confrontation can promote self-awareness and the development of identity as people learn through interpersonal actions. Democratization allows self-management to emerge and a certain altruism to flourish as one is allowed to contribute to the care of others. Communalism promotes interaction with others, sharing of responsibility, the abandonment of fixed social roles and attitudes and the development of new relationships.

What was very important was that most of the events which residents referred to as being significant during their treatment occurred within the community and in interaction with their peers (rather than staff members) and outside the actual 'therapy' groups. One ex-resident commented that:

The groups themselves weren't the place where things happened. They gave cerebral insights and stirred feelings up but it was during the unstructured times of the day, weekends, night time, down the pub, etc., when the intellectual insights of the day, week or month percolated down to the gut ... it was outside the group when things clicked into place. (Mahoney, 1979)

Also of importance to note, and seemingly in contradiction to principles of democracy and communalism, was the finding that those residents who benefited most were those who formed an attachment to the senior staff figures. It appeared that this attachment preceded improvement, rather than that those who benefited from the therapeutic community were then able to form attachments. In the normal process of personality development, John Bowlby and his colleagues have demonstrated the need for early attachment to stable 'parent' figures in order to grow towards independence and security and indeed to survive the inevitable losses that occur during a lifetime whether they be losses of family members or of relationships, of tangible objects such as jobs or possessions, or of more intangibles such as prestige, love or respect (Bowlby, 1988).

In another investigation, Norris (1983) was able to demonstrate how the individual changed his/her self-perception during the course of treatment, gaining in self-esteem and becoming more independent-minded while at the same time letting go of the old habits of delinquent behaviour as self-esteem grew and a defensive stance was relinquished. In the words of our earlier commentator:

I have proven to myself that I could accept responsibility and discharge it as I had done in the various jobs on the committee [monthly elected resident's committee] ... The Henderson had been the only place outside the family [Hell's Angels] where I had been given the opportunity to show what I could do, where people listened to what I had to say, where I was treated as somebody, as a person within my own right. (Mahoney, 1979)

A common pattern of passage through the therapeutic community was for new residents to embrace the unit and all it seemed to promise of a better life to come, but then to feel disappointed and even betrayed and duped when there was not immediate gratification. Some would leave at this point feeling that this was but a repetition of life's harsh treatment of them, but those who stayed with the therapeutic community, feeling supported by the new friendships gained through their participation in the process, would be the ones who gradually progressed to a less grandiose but more realistic outcome and were able to take their place in the outside world feeling less threatened and more self-reliant.

Applications of the therapeutic-community experience

We spend our lives in group situations, in the family, at school, in work and at leisure. What goes on between the members of groups will affect our behaviour more profoundly perhaps than what goes on inside our heads. One of the innovative psychotherapists involved in the therapeutic community at Northfield, S. H. Foulkes, developed from that situation his theory and practice of group analysis. He based this on the philosophy of treating the individual in his or her social setting where taking care of the group would take care of the individuals within the group, and participation in the group activity would be more important than the nature of the activity itself.

We have seen how the basic precepts of the therapeutic community are largely social processes. Their implementation evokes a capacity to manage change and overcome the anxiety associated with change. Openness of communication is needed to dispel mistrust and encourage participation in shared responsibility. Out of this can come opportunities for mutually supportive relationships to develop, altruistic acts to be performed and a corporate advance to be made with no question of one individual benefiting at the expense of another.

Therapeutic communities are social environments created for the purpose of helping people learn how to live together. Admittedly they are artificial environments, but no more so than schools, hospitals or workplaces, which are each designed for a purpose. The significance of therapeutic communities is that they represent a strand of human endeavour, going back some two hundred years but particularly marked during the last fifty, that has been working in we might call laboratory conditions on the question, 'How can we learn to live together?'

The social laboratory of the therapeutic community is far removed from the controlled environment of the research experiment. But the image is not totally fanciful. Irving Yalom (1985), the leading American writer on group psychotherapy, has used the metaphor of the social laboratory to describe what occurs in therapeutic groups. The value, and challenge, to the rest of us is to think about the practical relevance of these 'laboratory' findings to everyday life. Can we incorporate principles such as open communication, reality confrontation, democratization and the acceptance of shared responsibility in the way we live with each other? Would it help if we did? And if it would, how can we go about it?

References

Bowlby, J. (1988), *A Secure Base: Clinical Applications of Attachment Theory*, London: Routledge

Collis, M. & Whiteley, J. S. (1987), 'The Therapeutic Factors in Group Psychotherapy Applied to the Therapeutic Community', *International Journal of Therapeutic Communities*, 8, 1, pp. 21–32

Dickens, C. (1842), *Notes for General Circulation*, Chapman and Hall

Foucault, M. (1967), *Madness and Civilization*, London: Tavistock

Mahoney, N. (1979), 'My Stay and Change at the Henderson Therapeutic Community', in R. Hinshelwood, and N. Manning (eds.), *Therapeutic Communities: Reflections and Progress*, London: Routledge & Kegan Paul

Main, T. F. (1983), 'The Concept of the Therapeutic Community: Variations and Vicissitudes', in M. Pines (ed.), *The Evolution of Group Analysis*, London: Routledge & Kegan Paul

Norris, M. (1983), 'Changes in Patients during Treatment at the Henderson Hospital Therapeutic Community during 1977–81', *British Journal of Medical Psychology*, 56, 2, pp. 135–47

Rapoport, R. (1960), *Community as Doctor*, London: Tavistock

Rohman, D. J. (1971), *The Discovery of the Asylum*, Boston: Little, Brown & Co.

Whiteley, J. S. & Gordon, J. (1979), *Group Approaches in Psychiatry*, London: Routledge & Kegan Paul

Yalom, I. (1985), *The Theory and Practice of Group Psychotherapy*, New York: Basic Books

Chapter 2
FAMILY LIFE
Susie Orbach

Just one generation back, both my father, one of eight children, and my father-in-law, one of thirteen children, went to work at thirteen. My father who attended school until thirteen was the educated son. His brothers with little schooling were workers well before their voices had broken. At seventeen they went into the army where the fate of men befell them.

Long before they were thirteen, his sisters worked alongside their mother as aides in the emotional and domestic work of the family. The Edwardian or Victorian childhood introduced today to my children in school, a world of lollipops, toys and games, is a reconstruction, a nostalgic rewriting of the history. A history that pertained to children from selected families.

Whereas my father was one of eight children and my partner's father one of thirteen, we have only one sibling each and two children together. I stress this dramatic shift in family size in the space of one generation because in looking at families today, what they are for and what meanings they engender, we find that the family is not a fixed entity. The family has been in rapid flux at least since industrialization. War, work, emigration, unemployment and, recently, control over reproduction shape and reshape the family each generation. What my grandparents recognized as the family is at a great distance from the family I live in. For them the family was an economic and social unit, ruled by the emotional state of a patriarch. My grandparents left their country of origin to escape anti-Semitism and poverty and the whole family worked as a team to keep itself afloat. The family was a bulwark against society.

What my parents bequeathed me was an altogether different family. My father was the breadwinner whose life took place mostly outside the domestic milieu. That was masculinity then. My mother worked, but although her income was required it was treated, in the vernacular of the day, as 'pin money' which went to supporting her brother and mother. My mother had three jobs. One bringing up the children, the second running the household, the other teaching adults English. That was femininity then. Power within the family was not vested in the father; indeed it was the mother who was the authority figure. It was only when all else failed that, 'I'll tell your father and we'll see what he thinks about this,' would be uttered. A father might be proposed from time to time as a final arbiter but not necessarily a more authoritarian or punitive one.

In my family, there is yet another shift. The family is not a retreat from the world but a source of support for engagement with the world. My partner and I both work and contribute economically to the household. Masculinity and femininity are not determined by economic activity but by psychological development. The domestic duties and child-rearing are shared. This is not unusual for my generation. Many of my friends live in similar arrangements while others are raising children on their own or share children with a separated partner. Some live in blended families. In school, my children encounter even more variety. For them a family is a living group. Biology has a place in their notion of family but the physical and emotional arrangements of friends' living situations are what they denote as family. There is no stigma attached to 'singles' as they call them and no idea that the family must be one way.

I say this to root out a confusion. As psychotherapists, we know that whatever structure we grow up in will have enormous significance and meaning for us. It will live on inside us, affecting many of the activities we engage in and many of our emotional responses for the rest of our lives. But the overarching influence of early experience needs to be separated out from the form of that experience. In responding to the governmental call to strengthen the family and family values, we need to sort out what belongs where and not to conflate the emotional, material and spiritual needs of individuals and groups of people with a form that may or may not be necessary to meet those needs.

As Britain recognizes its shifting place in the global economy, as it comes to terms with its demise as an economic and political power, the image of Imperial Britain as father and mother to the world has to change. The metaphor of the mother country, as the place of safety and homecoming while the father marauds the world, is as inappropriate for modern Britain as is the picture of two parents, father at work, mother at home looking after the 2.2 children, to the family today. Neither conforms to our social reality. Our social landscape is filled with diversity and experiment, some of it born of necessity in the face of the changing economic and social conditions, some by choice. What psychotherapists can contribute to an understanding of families is not to reinforce the form but to disseminate what psychological processes prepare people for the demands of our society today. Psychotherapists have useful things to say about what makes relationships, families and outside life endurable. What makes people robust, engaged and adaptable.

The discipline from which my work derives – psychoanalysis – depends upon the production and reproduction of childhood and the family for its saliency. For many psychotherapists, examining childhood, masculinity, femininity and parental influence is part of what we do while at work. We help people read themselves retrospectively, understand themselves through the influences on them as gendered children and through their childhood initiatives and responses. This lens on childhood as development, and the emphasis on the emotional and sexual life of children and adults, and its significance, are important ways the twentieth century has begun to give an account of itself. Paradoxically as the world has become larger, as culture has become industrialized in every way, the Western world has defined itself in ever smaller units with the individual and the family as sacrosanct. Where Darwin's project was to understand the links in the biological world, the links between species, between flora and fauna, Einstein's to understand the links between the science of mechanics and of electricity and magnetism in the physical world, Marx's to understand the links between human autonomy, action, economics and the influence of history, Freud's project was to understand the links between the social experience of the child and the way this was represented and processed internally.

Freud took as his subject the child, later the infant, inside the adult, as he endeavoured to create a theory of human sexual and emotional development and psychic structure. Freud insisted that what occurred in childhood[1] could be extrapolated from the analysis of adults. Childhood, albeit once removed, was on the agenda as a science.

Freud's daughter Anna, Melanie Klein, Piaget, Winnicott, Kagan, Freiburg, Stern, Main, and thousands of workers have looked directly at childhood and the mind of the child. The space Freud opened up to look at childhood has over the last hundred years grown with acceptance. We now regard childhood as an experience of enormous significance and childhood needs are particularized. The cultural contract includes a general concern for the health, education and welfare of the child. In fact, even though it is a very recent idea, it is so much part of our sense of ourselves as products of a culture that we don't question it. We don't question what it is for, what we are doing, what underlying assumptions about human nature we bring to our study or management of childhood.

Childhood of course is intricately linked to the idea of family. The family is the setting for childhood and in recent years parenting groups have begun to focus on not just the needs of the child but the needs of parents and the wider context in which needs can be met. Many agendas have arisen, involving calls for more flexible work structures and an end to the madness that sees some people desperately overemployed (at both ends of the economic scale) while others are chronically unemployed. There are demands for decent, universal child-care, for parental leave, not just around birth but around school holidays, children's illnesses and so on.

In recent years we have seen two trends seemingly at odds with one another. On the one hand, we have seen many men desirous of active engagement with their children. On the other hand, we can observe men refusing the family and the support of their biological children. These counterpoised trends are interesting and perhaps less confusing if we fold into the picture the differing economic circumstances of men who are actively parenting and men who are not. The men of my generation and younger able to embrace parenting are by and large men who are or have been economically acknowledged, whose masculinity in the form of wage earning has been confirmed and who are able either to add child-rearing to their activities or to substitute it for work outside the home because that latter possibility has existed for them. By contrast the men deserting or choosing not actively to father are often those whose masculinity has had no economic confirmation. Where fathering equates with a masculinity that means economic provision to the family, the inability to create that provision creates a collapse in fathering as a practice or at the very least makes it problematic.

We no longer have a consensus about what constitutes parenting, mothering or fathering. Nor do we have a consensus about what a child's place is and how it is to achieve that place, or what constitutes the proper relations between adults and children, parents and children, children and children. We are instead shaping family life anew, redefining masculinity, femininity and parental responsibility, as well as parental rights and children's rights. Families for all of us are a less static concept. There is no straightforward progression from family of origin to independence and the making of one's own family. The permutations are infinite. Some children will stay within the family home and bring their new attachments to it; others will leave home and start their own families; some will raise children on their own; some will choose not to reproduce. Some households will contain a mix of three or four generations. In this *mélange* childhood and its place and purpose are somewhat wobbly. We aren't sure that we can give an account of what childhood is or should be and, if we have a desired ideal, how we might achieve it. We have some understandings of childhood gone wrong, but that is very different from an idea of what childhood gone right might mean. Sometimes we rush to fill the gap with nostalgic pictures of the family of yesteryear, where order was all and everyone knew their place. In conjuring up that idealization we screen out much of what is in the historical record as well as much of what we know from our own experience – the parts of the family that didn't speak to one another, Uncle Johnny's violence, the shame Jane brought on the family, the poverty, the child labour and so on. The nostalgic picture temporarily comforts us but at the same time it prevents us from grappling with the many realities that exist today, especially in regard to children and childhood.

Today we face a multiplicity of images, fragments of possibilities and eventualities about childhood. In my work as a psycho-therapist, I encounter violence within the family. I learn about the penetration of children's bodies by adults in perverse acts. I learn about torture and abuse. I know too of that which is not deemed to be abuse but represents itself as such in the minds of our adult patients: boarding school, fever hospitals, neglect, instances of unwanted separation or deprivation of parents which created a sense in the child that it was unloved, unwanted, unworthy. I hear about desperation and longing that has gone unmet.

Outside my practice I carry another set of images. These are benevolent. Rosy cheeks, cosy reading around the fire. Childhood is warm and toasty, a lovely place, a protected space, full of nice smells and comforting. Imagery that humanizes the adults, puts a smile on our faces, reminds us what it's all about. Good enough mothering.

There is also tragic imagery. Children dying before their time. Children losing their parents in Sarajevo, in the concentration camps. Children begging. Children starving.

And there is an imagery of children as malevolent, glue sniffing, marauding, out of control. The children who killed the toddler James Bulger, who killed the head teacher Philip Lawrence. The children who by their deeds, their attitudes, their enactment of the violence of the adult world, make us question what we think childhood is and what it is for.

As a clinician I hear stories about the *experiences* of childhood and the family. With my patients, I form pictures of the social structure of the family, the psychology of the parents, the inner life of the person who was once a child and who carries the imagery of their parenting inside them. I can theorize about the reproduction of psyches, of the transmission of pain from one generation to another, of the way in which emotional neglect, emotional brutality, emotional frailty, emotional fear, transmutes and transforms itself intergenerationally. Often, when I am sitting in the psychotherapist's chair, ironical thoughts arise in my mind about how childhood exists for the parents, not for the children. It is there for parents to work out their own difficult childhood. Parenting gives adults a chance to transform, to relive, to experience from a different vantage point the nature of childhood, to understand retrospectively the pressures on *their* parents, and to see the meaning of their own childhood in new terms.

I can observe what happens when family dynamics hurt children, when parenting goes awry. Behind this statement of mine of course is an assumption about parenting going right, about optimum childhoods and acceptable childhoods.

But there is no consensus about what constitutes the proper conduct towards children, about whether children are little people or whether children are something different. There are many conflicting views in our society about children; about the child–parent relationship, about children's rights, parental responsibilities, about whether children are their parents' chattels, to be married off in accordance with their parents' wishes, to work in jobs their parents deem appropriate, or whether children should be making their own way, with a right to create their own value system.

We don't have a consensus about whether it is acceptable to hit children or not. We don't have a consensus on what kinds of information children should be privy to, whether their emotional life is worth valuing, where sex fits in, where violence. Some see childhood as innocent, as a time to protect children, others recognize that very young children are dealing with the complex fall-out of society's social and economic arrangements, that children's emotional lives are every bit as passionate, violent and intense as the fairy tales that they listen to.

All of this is to say that while we have a set of practices we bring to parenting, we don't have a theory of childhood; we work with ideas which are often unarticulated, inconsistent and may often conflict with those of educators, politicians, capitalists and the very people we work with in therapy, adults. If we had a more unified view of what childhood is for, we might have a different way to evaluate the various practices that surround it.

Nor do we have a theory of parenting. We have ideological positions, we have unconscious ideas about what is a mother, what is a father; we have conscious ideas about adequate parenting and bad parenting. We have the experience of parenting, the agonies and the ecstasies of parenting, we can observe the emotional needs we bring to our children and to this role. But as a culture we often fail to evaluate what has been understood either about parenting, families or children.

Into this vacuum, psychoanalysis may have something to bring. Psychoanalysis has argued that childhood experience is formative. That what happens in early life determines the ways in which people will process their experiences and their attitude towards their wider environment.

Part of what psychoanalysis allows us to see is that when the early environment can provide relationships in which the developing child can have its initiatives responded to with care, when the needs of the child can be held in mind and thought about in ways which convey to the child the essential OK-ness, the legitimacy of its desires – that is to say of its very essence – the child grows up with the emotional base to be a partner in creating and maintaining attachments which are secure and stable. It can manage inside of itself the consequences of disappointment, of things going wrong.

The original relationships which surround a developing child can be thought of as the food for emotional growth. If the food is reasonably nutritious, the child will thrive. It will have absorbed the flow between itself and others as benevolent and it will have internalized a self-regard which allows it to engage with its wider environment with a confidence about its capacity to manage its needs, its interests and the disappointment of them.

In our earliest relationships, we absorb a mass of information about the world we are born into. Depending on our particular circumstances we take in the sense of whether differences between people can be managed, whether emotional responses can be textured and complex or are required to be monochrome, about inequalities and differences. We also learn something about our own impact, our agency. We sense what it is about us that can bring pleasure, can evoke responses in others. We don't process these phenomena at a conscious level, but the prolonged period of language and motor development, the fact that human beings only develop recognizably into what we call human within the context of relationships, indicates the crucial nature of early life.

Where early life fails to give the individual the recognition and relating that it requires, offers relationships in which needs go not so much unmet as unrecognized, the individual's development is marked by inner conflict. Not knowing or understanding whether it is their *need* that has made the other unresponsive or that it is their very *self* which has discouraged the contact that is required, she or he will experience a lack of self-regard along a continuum from insecurity to self-hate. The hurtful relationships cannot be left or given up and more satisfactory ones gone on to. The unsatisfactory relationships are manacles which may bind the person not only to the original relationships but to the shape and emotional pith of that original relationship for evermore. To put it starkly: if *satisfactory* relationships in early life incline one to seek out their repetition, so does the influence of *unsatisfactory* relationships. We are disposed to repeat what is, even if that has been felt to be insufficient, for that is how inside ourselves we experience relationships. We know no other way.

Where early relationships have been problematic several

processes are set in train. There is an invisible withdrawal from the world of actual relationships. People look like they are relating quite ordinarily – they have lovers, they play, work, procreate, etc. – but a part of them is split off and preoccupied with internal relationships. In these internal relationships, which analysts like to call object relationships – both to distinguish them from actual relationships and to demonstrate that they are relational scenarios which are available for psychic manipulation inside our heads – the person repositions her or himself not so much as a passive victim of circumstances but as a central actor in their own emotional drama. They hurt, they don't receive the love they need, they can't activate their energy and so on, because they haven't yet located the key that would render their love object and what they still require from their love object more available to them. In this process, it is not so much that they are powerless as uninspired. They haven't yet come up with what it is they need to do to instigate what they want from the other.

One aspect of this preoccupation with internal relationships can be a process of searching to please the other and by so doing restoring it to value so the other can in turn be giving. This, however, involves a further adhesion to a problematic relationship configuration. The extent to which the object has failed the person is in direct proportion to the level of its idealization. The greater the disappointment, the more unsatisfactory the relationship, the more, in the unconscious, is that person wanted. Meanwhile in the outside world, the experience of disregard or of unsatisfactory relating will predispose the person unwittingly to seek, attract and confirm that experience in new relationships, even as they try to challenge it. The channels for receiving that which doesn't meet the expectations are closed.

Internalized bad relationships then can't easily be given up. They are hard to digest and be done with. They linger and fester, unleashing emotional havoc on others, binding up psychic energy. Relationships are problematic and engagement in the world is often reactive rather than creative.

Now I say all this to stress that we have learnt a great deal about the enabling and disabling aspects of relationships. This is a critical contribution that psychoanalysis and psychotherapy has to make to an understanding of what human beings make of what they are given. Understanding in detail what enables or disables relationships is a far richer and more substantive offering than a call to a specific *form of relationships*.

What we require as individuals, as groups of individuals, as a society, are relationships which provide us with an emotional security. Emotional security is the basis of autonomy. Particularly in times of rapid unmapped change, the capacity to embrace what is, to think and to act out of that thoughtfulness, depends upon the internalization of enabling attachments.

Emotional dependency and autonomy are central to an understanding of human resilience, creativity and agency. Autonomy grows out of emotional relatedness; it is a consequence of a reasonable attachment.

We need not be mystified about what makes enabling relationships. Relationships that enable are those which allow for a full experience of the other, which allow for a range of emotional responses to be registered rather than interfered with. Enabling relationships depend upon parents being able to receive their children's feelings rather than denying them. To do this, adults have to have regard and respect for their own feelings in an equal emotional exchange with other adults. This can translate into being able to ask of another how they are and manage to stick around for a genuine reply without trying to fix, transform, deny or ridicule the responses they get. Enabling relating depends on a certain level of emotional literacy; the capacity to resonate with another emotionally without being swamped, to empathize without feeling impelled to make better, to register one's personal emotional responses in all their subtlety, so that there is space for those responses so often disregarded because they are insufficiently undramatic. Enabling relationships depend upon a mutual emotional exchange and a certain emotional fluency. Enabling relationships sustain us in the complexities of our responses. They make it possible for us to hold contradictory feelings simultaneously rather than retreat into an emotional fundamentalism where all is good or bad or all is love or hate and where scapegoating – projecting – dominates our relation to self and others.

This is what I mean when I say we do well to address the content rather than the form of familial relationships. Because if we can begin to take in what psychoanalysis has learnt about human psychological development, about what makes for the embrace of the world and what makes for the destructive acting out on it, what makes for the emotional capacities we require, we can offer a kind of thinking to policy-makers that reaches the parts that social reform guided only by economic, social and political considerations fails to get to. We can enhance policy by understanding what it is that provokes our individual and social responses, both at a private and a public level.

As psychotherapists, we are at the sharp end of the emotional illiteracy that bedevils our culture. We know from our personal experience the cost of psychic pain. Few of us will have entered such a profession with an A in mental health – indeed many of us will have sought professional training because we were ourselves in emotional difficulty. We then in our professional capacities work with people whose emotional pain has become serious enough for them to require help. We spend our days or our evenings listening to painful stories of distress and we recognize that we have the resources and skills to help those individuals through their distress and out the other side of it.

Few of us will not have reflected on the roots of the distress. Some of these roots are obviously economic, some political, some social. We have noted patterns in our clients' lives which create emotional difficulties. We have observed how when certain forms of emotional expression are denied, when particular feelings are not tolerated or named, when conflicts can't be talked about, when anger is denied, when power is exploited, when childhood vulnerability is abused, then the person grows up with fear, little secure sense of self, deep feelings of unentitlement and a bravado or fragility to cover the feelings of instability. We've observed how people search for soothing through drink, food, drugs. How destructive relationships become compellingly attractive.

Where clinicians have a consensus is that the routes of distress come from childhood and that childhood damage is hard to reverse. We know the cost of things going wrong and we know from our practices how to create the spaces for repair, to try to set things to rights again. So what would we recommend, what would we wish to institute as good practice if we wished to create the conditions in which childhood were different? If it had as one of its goals to grow up emotionally literate people, people who have the capacity to contain, process, digest and explore their emotional lives, so that instead of their feelings being a trouble to them, they are an integrated aspect of self, nourishing them and helping them through life rather than girdling them in an internally embattled state?

We would need to start at the beginning both before a baby is born and when the baby arrives. We need to extend the useful information parents get about changing nappies or preparing for labour with an emotional primer about parenting and a space for parents to think about the feelings that are aroused in them as they go about parenting. Parenting is the most momentous emotional experience both for parent and baby and yet it is the one we are prepared for only by our own experience of being parented. This is grossly insufficient. If we were to create a policy document about preparation for parenting, we could make extensive recommendations for what kinds of practices the area health authorities should institute ranging from emotional preparation for the baby, what the baby's emotional needs are, what emotional background facilitates baby's sleep, feed and prospering. But this would not be to exclude the needs of the parent or parenting situation. Part of what psychoanalysis understands can make parenting so very difficult are the feelings, the dramatic emotional states, stirred up in those parenting by the children. Spaces to explore and discuss such feelings can help both with the isolation that often accompanies parenting as well as enabling parents to sort through some of their emotional responses. In addition the feelings of siblings, the guilt of a parent or parents towards an older child, the loss of the couple relationship, the place of grandparents and so on rarely get aired straightforwardly. Parenting is, for most of us, a continuing education. Making provision to create the structures in which parents can reflect on their parenting, assimilate good practice, be given spaces to think about their children, their childhood and the kind of parenting they wish to be offering could be enormously valuable.

In this endeavour we would not be stressing the form of relationships as the content of relationships. We would draw upon what we understood about psychological processes and the varied ways in which emotional needs can be responded to and acted upon. We would be cognizant of the broader economic and social factors that construct the individual and the individual family. This contribution, which would start prenatally at one end of the cycle would become part of the child's educational experience at the other end of the cycle. As the child went to school it would enter an increasingly emotionally literate environment, one that respected its emotional development and needs as well as that of the teachers. Emotional respect would be both part of the ambience as well as part of the curriculum.

In this period of rapid global change, emotional attachments are at the core of an enlivened human existence. For attachments to be enabling and benevolent rather than disabling and destructively adhesive, we need to reflect upon the texture and quality of relationships. It is the texture and quality of relationships that make embrace of others and the world possible, not the form. For the word family to make sense to us it must transform itself from the site of ideology to a place of secure attachment for all its members.

Note

1. I am leaving aside the relevance of the actual events versus the fantasized events, since both positions can be accounted for in Freud.

Commentary
FAMILY FUNCTION

Susie Orbach's message is clear: family is as family does, not as family looks. It is the function of a family to provide its younger members with the kinds of experiences that enable them to grow up secure in themselves, able to 'read' their own and other people's feelings, and embrace and engage with a rapidly changing world from a position of autonomy. If a family can do this, says Susie, its particular form is irrelevant. Biology 'has a place', but the standard picture of the average family (both biological parents with their children, father at work, mother at home) is as out of date now as images associated with the British Empire in its heyday. We are not sure if that is true – yet – although it may well be in another generation. An Edwardian history book could open with the statement: 'The British Empire is the greatest fact the world has ever known.' Assertions about 'the family' have not yet reached that sense of hearing a voice from a different planet.

The more serious point is what *are* the essentials of a family? Are any and all arrangements for child-rearing OK? Is there a contradiction when Susie says on page 21 that 'whatever structure we grow up in will have enormous significance for us', and then a little later that it's the content not the form of the family that matters. A simple, incontestable understanding is that different forms *can* work equally well. Many children are successfully brought up by grandparents, foster parents or in adoptive families. More controversially this could be interpreted as saying that 'family' = 'living situation', so whoever you happen to be with, that's your family, which feels quite rootless. When Susie poses the question, 'What form of family is necessary to meet the emotional, material and spiritual needs of the individual?' the answer is not '2 + 2.2', but neither is it 'this month's partner'. It is whatever physical and emotional arrangements provide a sufficient basis for secure attachments. And the particular form those arrangements take cannot be predicted and should not be prescribed.

Susie Orbach writes in such a direct, personal way it comes as a bit of a shock when she goes into more technical language, or throws in a deceptively simple but reverberating statement like 'masculinity and femininity are not determined by economic activity but by psychological development'. One of the things we want to try to do is to 'unpack' the more technical part as well as respond to some of her seemingly simple ideas, which can be profound in their implications.

Susie begins with her own experiences of changes in family life as an example of the much wider changes in what we call 'family'. Every life is particular and as a grandchild of Jewish immigrants Susie's experiences would have been different from many of her contemporaries. The immigrant family had little choice but to work as a team, to be a bulwark against society. Transplanted to a new community, it lacked the wider support of relatives, friends and neighbours. Yet, whatever your own origins, your family has almost certainly known uprooting, hardship and poverty within the last three or four generations. You've led a charmed life if that is not the case for you. For most of us our own experience of family life is very different from our grandparents' experience. We can recognize some if not all the changes Susie describes from the team-against-adversity to the clear-cut distinction between father's role – breadwinner and final authority – and mother's – child-rearing and home-making – to joint salaries and housework. It's not that the distinctions between mothers and fathers have gone, but that a much wider range of patterns now exists, all the way from the old traditional divisions to full

34

economic and domestic equality, and all stations in between. Susie goes so far as to suggest that an individual's psychological development has replaced work as the main determinant of feminine/masculine status – at least in her own family. Perhaps economic support is no longer the main reason women look for a partner in our society, but there is still plenty of evidence that economic activity matters to men. Susie notes that men who have not been 'economically acknowledged' are more likely to refuse to take an active role in fathering. Later in this book Eric Miller reports that unemployment in the 1980s often led to a collapse of both self-esteem and sexual potency in former mine and factory workers. This suggests that economic activity is still very much with us as an influence on the man's role in the family, but perhaps in an interestingly paradoxical way. Doing the traditional male thing in one area – breadwinning – gives a man enough security in his masculinity to be less stereotypically male in other areas – e.g. in being more fully involved in child-care.

Alongside this major theme concerning the essentials of the family Susie also addresses a number of other issues. She points out that childhood itself has only been taken seriously as a subject of study in the twentieth century. We know a lot about children's physical needs for normal growth, about the child's cognitive and learning development, and we recognize that children have rights as individuals. Yet in the area of emotional development we know more about what goes wrong in childhood than about how to help it go right. Psychotherapists, who spend most of their working time with people whose childhood went wrong in some way, have developed theoretical models of how we develop the capacity to form relationships. One of these theories uses the picture of internal objects (as in 'you are the object of my desire' rather than 'this is an interesting object'), and in explaining this Susie demonstrates the highly technical nature of much psychoanalytic theorizing.

Object Relations Theory proposes that our relationships can be with external 'objects' (i.e. actual people) or with internal 'objects'. Internal objects can be described as mental images of others, derived from earlier external relationships, that we react to as if they were real. Without usually being aware of it we bring these images into new relationships. We look for, or expect to find, people who resemble our images. So, for example, if our internal image is of a hard-to-please parent, in a new relationship we can find ourselves relating to this image rather than to the actual person. Misunderstanding and conflict in relationships are often of this kind because the relationship is being carried on not only between two actual people, but also between each person and the mental image they have of the other. If the mental images don't fit there will be a pressure to change them and for the partners to see one another as they really are. If there is quite a good fit with the other person's character – say the other person really is like a hard-to-please parent – the relationship may continue without either noticing that they are relating to the other more as an image than as a real person. In benign situations no one minds this. Two people in love can be like this. Each sees the other as their dream come true. In malignant situations the opposite happens – the other is one's living nightmare. These are the cases that psychotherapists often see. When Susie talks of a further adhesion to a problematic relationship configuration, we can take her to mean getting stuck or caught once again in a relationship of this kind.

Theories about how relationships go wrong are complex and useful in psychotherapy. But how do we judge what will make things go right as parents or family-makers? We tend to fall back on nostalgic images of childhood because all else we have to guide us is our own experience of being parented and this, according to Susie, is 'grossly insufficient'. Can that really be so? After all it must be what guided previous generations, back into antiquity. The difference perhaps is in the insecure and changing nature of society so that inner security matters more than it did when roles and jobs were fixed for life.

One way forward might be to try to develop a unified theory of childhood and parenting. Could there be one? And if there were, could we avoid it becoming an ideology? Could diversity of family forms still be allowed to flourish? Later in the book we will see what other contributors have to say about living with uncertainty and the risks of ideology. What is proposed in the heart of Susie's essay is 'food for growth'. This is a metaphor of the child's emotional environment: the emotional response the child gets to its initiative and desires will nurture or wither it. The well-nurtured child will grow up secure and autonomous, the poorly nurtured child insecure and compelled to go on repeating a pattern of failing relationships. This simple, compelling hypothesis leads Susie to make the case for a national approach to creating the conditions for good parenting.

This argument brought a mixed response from our discussion group: 'Sensible', 'good simple ideas', 'there are already lots of primers around', 'oppressive', 'too prescriptive', 'I'd rather take my chances.' We quote these because this range of responses is likely anywhere you take these suggestions. It is the problem of how to make use of a good theory without turning it into an ideology where dissent becomes heresy. Our century has seen enough of social-engineering projects to be wary of that. Yet left to ourselves, making a botch of parenting is all too common.

Can we improve the way families, in whatever form, function to provide the emotional nutrition we need? And in trying to achieve this is it possible to overstate the case for the family as the make-or-break factor in everyone's lives? What other sources of security, autonomy and self-respect are available in our society? These are questions that other contributors to this book will try to address.

Chapter 3
CHILDREN OF DIFFERENT ENGLANDS
Valerie Sinason

'Boys and girls come out to play
I call you up now
I am marking the register
of broken nursery rhymes
Are you there?
Are you truanting dear dead ones?'

Valerie Sinason 'Round Up', 1986

Within one block of flats in one street in London there are
countless different lives being lived. While the external structures
of bricks and mortar, historical time, geography, shared dangers,
shared scenery, access to mass media are common and provide an
Esperanto, there are also astounding differences.

When we wonder what it is like for a child to be experiencing pre-millennium England or hazard hypotheses about post-millennium life, which child are we considering?

Are we considering a particular real-life child who haunts us outside of treatment hours, whose living conditions come straight from a Dickensian underclass; a child whose lack of good-enough attachment figures means she lives in a tragically depleted world where there is no justice or sense of safe continuous time? Are we considering the average resilient-enough child capable of representing something about the current way of life? Is the child a projected aspect of our own psyche – the child we fantasize we would be if we were a child now? And what social class does this child come from? Class, living conditions, nature of attachment and attachment figures, religion, gender, intelligence and health all affect what kind of England and what kind of time can be experienced.

Twenty years ago as a young housewife with two small children, I was invited into a rich upper-class neighour's house. Our children attended the same nursery school and were close friends. However, while her children regularly saw me at the start and end of morning nursery, I never saw her. It was always the nanny, called 'Nanna', who collected them. My five-year-old son liked his friends' nanny. They've got a Nanna like me he said happily. His 'Nanna' was my mother, who, like her own mother before her, had chosen that term as her favoured grandmotherly title. Nevertheless, he had understood, from his subjective experience, that there was an emotional as well as linguistic similarity between the two nannas that counted more than difference.

At the appointed time we rang the bell of the imposing house and a uniformed maid ushered my children away from me to join their friends. I was informed that, 'Nanny will give the children tea in the nursery.' I was taken into a magnificent dining room where my neighbour greeted me and a procession of dishes were brought in while I heard about the difficulties in the cost of living and how hard it was to have good servants nowadays. I was finding it hard, in the absence of our children, to find subjects in common. When I, at some point, made a lame comment about how lucky we were nowadays in the West to have such items as washing machines and hoovers my neighbour commented, 'Oh no – if we had lived in the past our servants would have done it.'

Perhaps it was that moment more than any moment in my later professional work as a teacher and then a child psychotherapist that highlighted for me what different Englands each of us inhabits, even if we are living in the same neighbourhood in the same moment of history. Our sense of the kind of past our ancestors had and our equally projected fantasies of the future our children might have are therefore dependent on our own experiences initially.

With each child and adult I have worked with as a teacher and psychotherapist I am aware that whatever Esperanto we share as humans there are enormous individual differences. To attune properly to one another and understand each other's language and subjective experience are essential. From my own mixed-class upbringing I became aware of external signs of living conditions that also reflected inner states of mind.

From five to sixteen I lived in different council estates from King's Cross to Plumstead. In 1950, in my King's Cross primary school in London there were children without shoes, only partially clothed. In 1958 in south east London, middle-class children from my school were not allowed to visit me. Class prejudice was a two-way process. In a poem, 'Family Tea' (*Inkstains and Stilettos*, 1986), I wrote of childhood visits to a middle-class aunt. The extract below shows the way different styles were misperceived.

> At her house
> it smelled of carpets – everywhere
> her tomatoes were thinly sliced
> her white bread was thinly sliced
> Sugar cubes lay in a silver bowl
> milk rested in a silver jug
> and fancy biscuits (two each)
> were geometrically arranged on a china plate
>
> So much fuss for so little, we thought
> In the language of our class she was mean and showy.

My parents' progression to middle-class life and home ownership in a suburb when I was sixteen meant that the homes I visited and the teenagers who visited me had very different backgrounds. As a result of such sharp class experiences I find I have a keen eye for it professionally. As a school psychotherapist in Tower Hamlets in a school for emotionally disturbed adolescents I was part of a staff group that automatically provided tea and toast in the morning, knowing that many of the children had not been given any breakfast. I delayed the start of therapy sessions to fit in this crucial breakfast time. I also became aware as a teacher and therapist that a child could remain in school blazer or coat not because they were unwilling to settle in the class or therapy room but because they were deeply shamed by holes or frayed areas in second-hand clothes or clothes their parents were too depressed to clean. Here is an extract from a poem 'That Child' based on my teaching experience.

> That child in the back row
> tired from the paper round
> sips his school milk
> and shrinks.
>
> His book is open at the wrong page
> It is the wrong book too.
> He fills his pen with failure
> A slow inkstain covers all.
>
> I am looking at the stars of skin
> that stare through his shirt
> and never shine.

It also became easier to understand when adolescents were shaving their heads out of despair and anger, and transforming it into a uniform, from when there was a proactive attempt to avoid the shame of headlice.

It can be seen that the child I am most concerned for, living in England now and after the millennium, is the vulnerable one. The incomes of the poorest 10 per cent fell by 14 per cent in real terms between 1979 and 1991 according to the Households Below Average Income survey. Barnado's and Youth Aid found that young people receiving hardship payments (published figures 23 March 1993) increased from 10,669 in 1989–9 to 77,906 in 1991–2; 45 per cent of those claiming severe hardship payments had slept rough and 22 per cent had been physically or sexually abused by parents or residential workers. One quarter of MORI's survey were classed as young offenders and a link was shown between offending and lack of benefit entitlement.

But perhaps one of the most painful statistics of English child life was that provided by Professors John and Elizabeth Newson at Nottingham University. They found that 63 per cent of mothers hit their babies under one year old. Even more hit their four-year-olds and 7 per cent of these four-year-olds are hit at least once a day. By the age of seven, 22 per cent have been hit with an implement (29 per cent in social classes one and two) and 53 per cent have been threatened with an implement; 75 per cent of all seven-year-olds (91 per cent of boys and 62 per cent of girls) had been hit or threatened with an implement. They found a clear connection between frequency of physical punishment at eleven and later delinquency: 'The measures that stand out as being more predictive of a criminal record before the age of 20 are having been smacked or beaten once a week or more at 11 and having had a mother with a high degree of commitment to formal corporal punishment at that age.'

From my experience in working with violent boys who have been excluded from school, the majority were being brought up with no father involved in their upbringing. The combination of worn-out mothers resorting to physical violence in the absence of support, yet also tantalizing their sons by sharing beds at the age of eleven, was starkly damaging. I consider we need to stop using the expressions 'single-parent family' and 'single mother' so emphatically and concentrate instead on the 'two-family child' or the 'one-parent child'. Housing departments need to allocate larger flats to families and ensure that shared beds at this age are not facilitated. Sons without fathers who are scared of their incestuous feelings (often provoked by their mothers) can themselves provoke physical violence to deal with their guilt. The mothers can be projecting their physical fury with the departed partner on to the son. This shared physical violence is aided by cultural acceptance of physical punishment in the home.

From 1950 to 1965, my school years, I witnessed brutality from teacher to child that would nowadays constitute physical abuse. I do think there has been an important transition period as a result of the legal abolition of corporal punishment within state schools. The concept of an instrument of pain as an 'educational' tool is no longer acceptable. We are now experiencing a painful discrepancy between knowledge that physical punishment is not a helpful way of rearing our young and the mental state of unsupported parents who do not feel able to find another mode of operating.

I hypothesize that as we move into the next century, so long as we do not have war to contend with and so long as there is no further economic decline, there will be a progressive lessening of physical punishment in the home. This will make school and home congruent again. Before it was the dictatorship of the teacher, the Wackford Squeers, and the child was the victim. Now the home is the place of violence and the school becomes the dictatorship of the oppressed where the teacher becomes the victim of class violence and is held in contempt for his lack of 'strength'. However, I hypothesize that this dislocation will lessen and will result in a reduction of bullying in schools and a breaking or fading of the cycle of physical violence.

Change can come from the outside and from the inside. As a psychoanalytical psychotherapist, I witness, where treatment is successful, the changes in perception that occur as a result of it. Millie, aged seven, began therapy saying, 'My house is dark. There are rats, mice, rubbish smells.' A few months later there was no improvement in her external conditions but internal change had occurred. 'My bed has got a bedspread with flowers on it. It is a pretty bed and we don't let the mice get on it.' In other words, her internal sense of having a private space that was aesthetic, protected and valued could be projected on to the external furnishings and make her more determined to fight them. It is a well-known fact in treatment that at a certain point of time patients consider their parents have improved!

An improvement in internal representations of parent figures can make for better relationships with the external ones. A physically and mentally disabled young woman began therapy terrified of going out and facing the gauntlet of aggressive responses on her estate. Her sense of being damaged and worthless was so strong she could not bear the mirror image of it in the estate. However, after a year's therapy she announced, 'The boys on my estate threw stones at me and called out "Spastic! Spastic!" I said to them, "That's right. I am spastic and you are lucky you are not. But you are rude boys and I am not rude."' In other words, there is a powerful continuous loop between what is happening externally, internally and the relationship between them.

While I have been deeply moved by the way external circumstances can be experienced differently when there has been internal change, I am equally struck by the impact positive and negative external circumstances have on internal life. In my work with children and adults with learning disability I have noted the way improvements in their living conditions and rights have led to greater numbers of painful disclosures about abuse. An improvement in the way our courts handle such vulnerable witnesses will, I am sure, continue into the next century, bringing forth more reminders of the secret damage that goes on in our community. Progress brings problems too. However, I have also been deeply struck by the powerful impact of negative experiences. Where sexual abuse is concerned, the adversarial nature of the courts or the failure of a case even to get to court destroy the victim's hope for justice.

Perhaps one of the most painful things I have learned from my work in the field of sexual abuse is that if we cannot consider the possibility of what a client may have suffered then they will not be able to mention it. I have also learned that I can only see what my own time span allows me to. My uncovering of abuse within the context of formal psychoanalytic psychotherapy follows the historical pattern. Abuse by male family figures came first, followed by abuse by mothers and others; females, animals, paedophile rings, satanist rings. Although I may be on a particular step of a time escalator with the company of trusted colleagues, I am very aware that with each new hurt that is uncovered a patient had to wait a considerable time for me to bear hearing it and there will always be a new one I have not yet faced.

Those with learning disability, formal mental illness and multiple personality who allege abuse and particularly ritual abuse are not adequately listened to and I suspect that, come the millennium, we will find abuse just as hard to bear. In fact, as the numbers of alleged victims continues to rise we are likely to find the reflection of our damage even more painful to look at. However, the more we are able to look into the experiences of pain, loss and perversion and deal with them the stronger we will become. A strong society will understand that it is damaged but can acknowledge its scars. Given the pain our species has suffered, it is a source of celebration that we are here to celebrate the millennium!

Commentary
BETTER THE DEVIL YOU KNOW

The first thing Valerie Sinason wants us to appreciate is that we know so little about other people's experience. Sometimes our ignorance lies in the area of social class differences and all that goes with that. Sometimes it is in the area of people's inner lives. In particular we may be oblivious to someone else's terrifying ordeal because they can only communicate this to someone who is ready and able to hear it. Valerie's wealthy neighbour who assumed that everyone had servants and the teacher or psychotherapist who assumes that the story the child is telling them must be made up are both caught in the same trap. Both screen out possibilities that would make them feel helpless, out of their depth, not knowing what to say or do.

Of course we all do this – screen things out – to an extent. We view the world in terms we are familiar with, trading real understanding for the comfort of having our assumptions confirmed. The bullying at school – he must be exaggerating. Sexual harassment at work – she is overreacting. Young people begging – they are just lazy. What Valerie is saying is that the more we can allow ourselves to recognize the pain that other people suffer – psychological or physical, by chance or because someone intended it – the stronger we will be.

Why should this be so? Is it not more likely that we will either become satiated with these accounts and emotionally 'switch off' (a response with its own label, Compassion Fatigue) or else get increasingly depressed and demoralized at our inability to make things better?

Perhaps Valerie's optimism can be understood in this way. The more we organize our lives on false assumptions the more likely we are to misjudge the effects of what we do, whether as an individual or a society. Such misjudgements weaken our real effectiveness. Examples abound of actions which were intended to help but were ineffective because judgements were based on false assumptions – large-scale examples, such as misjudgements by aid agencies leading to piles of useless drugs and equipment at famine distribution centres, and misjudgements by politicians and their advisers over food safety, leading to massive loss of consumer confidence; and small-scale examples, such as where a husband misjudges his wife's mood and tries to placate her when what she wants is an honest discussion, leading to increased not decreased discord, or where a social worker misjudges the safety of a child's home situation, leading to increased risk of abuse. The common point of these examples is that our actions can be more effective – better judged – if we don't assume we know the answer to a problem, indeed if we assume that we do not know the answer, and can tolerate the uncertainty of this and keep an open mind.

Valerie uses her own experiences as a child, mother and psychotherapist as a prelude to some striking statistics relating to poverty, abuse and offending in children and young people. These demonstrate connections between poverty and abuse, and between physical punishment at home and an early criminal record. Hitting or smacking may be an acceptable form of discipline within the culture a family exists in, or they may be the result of tensions and frustrations between a child and a parent who is feeling unsupported. Valerie describes both types of situation. She suggests that in either case cultural norms play an important role, and she offers a major prediction about a current trend within our society. Her prediction is that following the abolition of corporal punishment in schools, a cultural movement has been set in motion that is moving us away from seeing physical punishment as an accepted feature of child-rearing towards seeing it as an aberration. This will make its effects felt throughout our homes in the coming decade.

A long-running research study by John and Elizabeth Newson (1978), referred to by Valerie, interviewed the mothers of around 700 children born in Nottingham at the end of the 1950s and has followed the children at intervals since then. The findings Valerie quotes related child-rearing practices in the 1960s to criminal behaviour when these children reached their teens in the 1970s. Such studies have repeatedly confirmed, in the words of Sir William Utting (1996), that 'how children are treated ... is the key to their own behaviour'. What they cannot tell us is whether the use of corporal punishment on young children has remained the same over the past thirty years or has already begun to decline. If it has declined, it will be another twenty years before we can know what impact this may have had on violence and criminal behaviour in young adults.

If it *is* the case that a cultural shift is taking place, it also raises another important question for us as individuals and as a society. How do we learn to deal with the passions that relationships with those closest to us can arouse, especially those that can lead to violence? The dilemma in psychodynamic terms is that anger that is not directed at its original target will either be repressed (a source of potential physical stress), displaced on to another object (the son instead of the father in Valerie's example), or directed against the self in some kind of self-harm, including alcohol and drug abuse. All of these are unhealthy for the individual and for societies in which they become endemic. There must be some other way. One approach to this problem comes from a branch of psychotherapy known as cognitive therapy. This works on the premise that anger is connected with how we perceive and interpret events, and can be modified if we learn how to 'reframe' events. To give a simple example, if somebody pushes into us in the street our initial reaction may be one of anger. If we then notice that the person is blind, we reinterpret the event as unintended and our anger disappears. In personal relationships anger is often associated with one person misinterpreting the other's behaviour as a deliberate provocation, with escalating accusations leading to potentially disastrous consequences.

If society is changing in the direction that Valerie predicts, learning how to manage anger in ways that are neither self-destructive nor harmful to others could join up with Susie Orbach's suggestion for emotional literacy education to become as basic as training in road safety and first aid.

References

Newson, J. & Newson, E. (1978), *Seven Years Old in the Home Environment*, Penguin
Utting, Sir W. *et al.* (1996), *Children and Violence*, published by the Gulbenkian Foundation

Chapter 4
SMOOTH OPERATORS
ROB WEATHERILL

We must begin to love in order that we may not fall ill and must fall ill if, in consequence of frustration, we cannot love. (Freud, 1914, p. 69)

Ours is rather like the situation of a man who has lost his shadow: either he has become transparent, and the light passes right through him, or alternatively he is lit from all angles, and overexposed and defenceless against all sources of light. We are similarly exposed on all sides to the glare of technology, images and information, without any way of refracting their rays ... (Baudrillard, 1990, p. 44)

The continuous revolution

I want to start by making a number of assertions.[1]

1. There is now no recoverable form of *traditional* family life. The erosion of the extended family and social fabric in general has occurred over a long period, but most recently in two cultural revolutions. The first, during the 1960s when the family was regarded on the New Left as an 'ideological conditioning device' (Cooper, 1971), to be subverted and dispersed into a multiplicity of lifestyle forms. The second, during the 1980s in which the New Right emerged with radical economic freedom from social constraints – 'there is no such thing as society'. These revolutions followed on the devastating effects on family life and the social fabric of two world wars.

   It is not surprising, therefore, that some post-war British psychoanalytic theorists became intensely aware and concerned about the stability and reliability of the early familial environment for infant care in a culture that was already unravelling. The breakdown[2] of the family (more broadly, the end of traditional cultures worldwide under the impact of the modernizing process) leads to the loss of on-going living contact and cohesiveness between parent and infant, and also a loss in the continuous education and integration of the emotional life, which have long-term implications.[3] In a sense the ego itself is being lost for want of support in its formative years. We can no longer be sure of Bion's assertion that, 'like the earth, he [the child] carries with him an atmosphere, albeit a mental one, which shields him from the mental counterpart of the cosmic and other rays at present supposed to be rendered innocuous to men, thanks to the physical atmosphere' (Bion, 1992, p. 192).

2. Human solidarity, whether local, factory, class or familial, has disappeared. Since the end of the 1950s, we have noticed the beginning of the end of working-class movements, and the slow break-up of the body politic into competing groupings that ceased to define their interests in terms of a better society, but rather in competing terms of narrow self-interest and

claims of victimization. The collapse of the British miners' strike in 1984 was the last flicker of human solidarity. Now, each wants his individualized freedoms. Freedoms are the absolute good. Commitment has gone in favour of limited contractual relationships. The old restrictive bonds of the social have dissolved into a kind of kinetic energy of communication, networking and interactivity.

3. The excessive sexualization of culture makes what heretofore was implicit, repressed and hidden, now, explicit, de-repressed and excessively open. There is now more than ever the *absolute* seductiveness of modern *image* culture. The sexiness of everything: 'In our culture everything is sexualised before disappearing' (Baudrillard, 1983, p.55). Marcuse dubbed this *de*sublimation. There is nothing secret about sex any more. Adolescents may no longer come upon sexuality as a new and potentially enriching, indeed frightening experience, because it has for so long been a matter of media attention, entertainment and pornography. The forcing of sexuality everywhere in the media, in popular music, on access radio, hot lines, help-lines, information lines, etc., favours regressive solutions, acting-out, teenage pregnancies and the widespread feeling that condoms are the solution. Sexual activity is more and more used to fill a void, which in all former times was hidden and unknown.

We can no longer count on privacy, an inner reserve involving the capacity to sublimate. Privacy and reserve are regarded as almost pathological, and our reserves (inner and outer) are almost spent. We have lost a necessary fixity of personal boundaries. Ours is a culture of expression, of telling all, of sharing intimacies, preferably to mass readership, or television and radio audiences. Such intimate revelations are valued as courageous, honest and open. Privacy and reticence are now seen to be connected with inhibition, something to be slightly ashamed of.

Without boundaries, things can flow out of us and into us without restriction, or in terror of this possibility, we can erect boundaries of such intensity that nothing can get in or out.

This is most dramatically represented by the incidence of rape and child abuse. From this perspective, these crimes involve a break into the most primitive and therefore most essential defences which stand guard over our secret autonomy and unknownness. We correctly regard these crimes very seriously, because we are aware of these fundamental breeches. It is sexuality that symbolizes our privacy (the genitals are the private parts), and it is around sexuality therefore that invasions – both psychical and physical – will occur, in a culture of total openness.

4. No more depth. Orthodox psychoanalysis, coming as it has out of the modern tradition, has always understood some notion of defence against the more hidden or repressed unconscious formations. We have always understood that interpretation and free association would reveal something of the 'inner depth'. There would be a movement from surface to depth, from manifest to latent, from the false self to the true self, from ego to subjectivity, from persona to self, and so on. But all depth models have ended. Along with the opposition between latent and manifest, the distinction between appearance and essence, or the old existential notion of authenticity versus inauthenticity and alienation, or the opposition between signifier and signified, we have discovered there is at last *no* depth and *no* truth to uncover. In *post*-modernity, we know that there are only surfaces, plays of light, reflections, refractions, diffractions and language playing with itself This is also the end of psychoanalysis.[4] If there is no longer any solid real upon which to call, there must instead be endless reproductions of scenes, retrospections, scenarios, interminable streams of circulating imagery and discourse (interminable therapy) as a cover for the horror (at one time the secret) that there is nothing real at all.

The modern and postmodern exploration of nothingness of an absolute zero, of nihilism, which is the *excavated* centre around which we now revolve, cannot be discounted. Living now with a total and elated ephemerality, instability, illegitimacy, and an endless recycling of texts, with no *ultimate point of reference*, no authorization, and no longer any appeal to Logos, we have involved ourselves in a rigorous disillusionment against which there can be no trivial consolation and no appeal.

But, it is argued that such a radical denaturing of the modern self, such a pursuit of the last vestiges of meaning, is in itself an intensely ethical project, which owes a debt to the traditions which it at the same time is annihilating. Does it not call forth a movement, a radical concern, a desire to find new meanings beyond meaninglessness? Perhaps. However, any appeal to ultimacy on our part, or any other appeal to common sense, to the obvious meanings in life, or the traditional interpretive consensus, and so on, cannot refute the (deconstructionist) argument. It cannot be refuted on its own terms.

5. Nevertheless, in face of such radical nihilism and the general cultural pessimism of the West, there has been a counter-response – a cultural shift in favour of a maternal feminine completeness and harmony.[5] There is a drift or slide towards the maternal, towards a feminine ideality, where there is blurring of the distinction between formerly *differential* terms: conscious and unconscious, male and female, parent and child, right and wrong, and so on. These terms must lose their difference and their meaning, as do all terms within the soft embrace of the imaginary feminine principle of continuity and seamlessness – a magical world with no cut with *no* severance, the world of the ideal ego, of *indifference*. The belief here is that the feminine will heal everything.

The end of Oedipus

More specifically, I want to focus on an argument that I advanced in *Cultural Collapse* (Weatherill, 1994). Here I noted the broad cultural shift away from the psychoanalytic ideal of the heroic Oedipus towards the doomed Narcissus. Freud always maintained the centrality of the Oedipal conflict and its tragic outcome. With the dismantling of what we might call the old paternal super-ego, embodied in the social institutions of the church, family, police and school, children are left exposed to a more *immediate* and driven emotionality and the increased anxiety arising therefrom. Technically, with no effective external repressive forces to combat the id any more, new, more primitive defences must be erected to oppose primitive drives. These defences Klein (1933) referred to as the *archaic super-ego*, which paradoxically is much more brutal and punitive than the old super-ego it has largely replaced. Freedom from the old repressive taboos has meant *increased* levels of anxiety. All change brings anxiety, but this 'liberation' from all restraint has involved increasing numbers of children in an *excess* of anxiety. And we might connect this sort of psychoanalytic theorizing with well-known facts about children's suffering – increased eating disorders, juvenile crime, psychiatric admissions and at younger ages, drug abuse and underachievement at school.[6] Child-care professionals will tell you that levels of child distress are far greater than they were only a decade ago – more depressions, more behaviour problems and so on.

Things have changed so much that it is harder and harder to imagine Winnicott's (1963) ideal of infancy with the mother's provision of 'primary illusion' for her baby, deemed to be so important for what Winnicott calls our sense of aliveness and creativity. Winnicott said: 'I assume all the time a mother person holding the situation, day by day, weekly, week out' (1988, p. 78). The outcome, Winnicott tells us, is a transitional space – a neutral area of experience which will not be challenged' (1951, p. 239). Then comes a necessary *dis*illusionment beginning at weaning, and developing through inevitable losses, the reality principle, in Freudian terms, the introduction of a cut (symbolic castration) initiated by the father, which gives depth and what has been called 'affective density'. But to a degree this inaugural experience of primary illusionment stays with us as a partial *shield* against pain and loss. But the two movements are essential. On the one hand, to be in this private privileged erotic relationship with the mother (figure) which grounds the infant in its own special desirability and provides this illusion of security, and, on the other hand, the break-up of this, the failure, the unavoidably tragic loss of unity initiated by the father (figure), who will insert the child into the cultural order under the law. The child moves from having a supreme place to taking up a *limited place* within the social fabric. Destabilization of this formative Oedipal process[7] leads to emotional extremism, and to the beginning of the end of illusion, which made life bearable, even enjoyable. My point has been that this transitional space has collapsed into a frenzy of vapid gratification characteristic of the narcissistic personality, whose flatness, hyperactivity and emotional coldness are all there to seduce us away in *simulations* of self. Everything then has to be forced and confused into a near likeness of itself.

Poverty, (male) unemployment, marketization of the work-force, families without fathers, communities without fathers, fathers without fathers, have all contributed to this generalized collapse, which, in psychoanalytic terms, is the loss of the space of this mythical Oedipal period, which of necessity inscribes in us a *prophylactic* loss, guilt and a sense of indebtedness to the world. No one feels in debt any more. No one feels gratitude. Marriage was always there to bind men and women, however imperfectly, into the community. Through marriage the father was connected to the larger community, where he frequently became involved with teaching or instruction of the younger generation. Now, there is a new underclass of mainly working-class male youth, immature, unsocialized and withdrawn from any residual social structure. This is only the sharp visible end of a more generalized loss of the paternal function and any agreed notion of authority. Now, finally, we are all our *own* authorities.

But, some cultural historians suggest, that this is nothing new. Family life has been chaotic and distressful since at least the mid-eighteenth century. What is now the loss of a parent by divorce used to be loss of a parent by early death. In the nineteenth century there was concern about young men on the streets and what they might get up to, which was part of a general concern, then as now, about children in the large cities. Apprentices too, although looked after by a master – what happened to them when they went out on the street? Many will stress that our present concerns are not at all new.

However, when it comes to children's culture and

commodities aimed at children, most concede that socialization of children is really increasingly about a cynical expansion of corporate interests – the exploitation of children as consumers. No debt, no castration, but instant gratification – the (human) right to demand what they want and to be happy – now. The children's market in the US is worth a hundred billion dollars. There has been an immense corporate research effort to find out precisely what children want, to speak to them in their own language, to design toys and products that will exactly stimulate and gratify their desires. What is essential is 'product tie-in'. In the 1990s every new product is launched through TV – not through the ads, but the programmes themselves. In the 1980s in the US (not the UK), there was Reaganite deregulation of children's TV. Toy manufacturers were free to create and market identities and personalities for children to engage in fantasy with. They *amplified* the gender split: Action Man and the violent resolution of conflict; Sindy and Barbie, dolls who want to be attractive and be the centre of attention.

All this industry to fill an unbounded space opened up by spiralling demand free of any restraints.

Michael Rosen, the author of *The Penguin Book of Childhood*, suggests that there have been ads specifically aimed at children throughout the twentieth century, Dinkies, Meccano, etc. For Rosen, it is just a question of degree and volume. Neil Postman's book *The Disappearance of Childhood* has been reprinted after ten years. He points out that children were traditionally kept from the secrets of the adult world – intimate sexual and medical knowledge. This we understand, psychoanalytically, as the repression central to Oedipus. However, now, TV presents all these secrets. All generations watch the *same* soft pornographic world now. Therefore, there is no point any more in eavesdropping on adult conversation. But, say others, why should children have secrets withheld from them? Why in short should we insult them by treating them like children?

Even children's books, once thought to be safe and situated firmly in the transitional space, now have to deal with the gritty realities of homelessness, domestic violence, etc. At one time, children's literature explored the great themes, which took them out of their time and their immediate circumstances. Now, it is widely argued, children shouldn't be protected from what they see on a London street. Look at *Hansel and Gretel*: a story of two parents who want to kill their children, and another parent figure who wants to eat them up! This line of argument completely misses the point about the *symbolic* nature of so-called brutal fairy tales (see Bettelheim, 1976). But to push the point further, why not video games, with their very reduced narrative, the emotional hit, always unsatisfying, so you keep playing? And why not, moving towards the zero of narrative, channel-zapping, channel-surfing, from so-called three-minute culture to a-few-seconds culture? All this increasing fragmentation, acceleration and immediacy are essential to disperse the excessive effects unleashed by the end of Oedipus. The time is one of total restlessness, irritability on the edge of a fatal futility.

Our view of childhood has shifted decisively, in the modern period, from believing children to be bearers of Original Sin to seeing them as blessed with innocence and in need of protection. This shift is reflected in a complex way within psychoanalytic theorizing. The recognition of the perverse infantile sexuality that must come under the law of the father during Oedipus, versus the emphasis on holding, reverie and mothering and the creating of the transitional space that we have noted above.[8] Modern children were to be cherished. This shift began with the middle class and then spread to the working classes – children working in cotton factories, in chimneys, in mines, were all seen as being at odds with nature. Intense campaigning for reform in the late nineteenth century and early twentieth century resulted in children being excluded from adult working environments, from public houses, etc. They were felt to be too exposed to the adult pornographic world. Enclosures were made for them – safe havens, playgrounds, schools, special zones.

But this couldn't last. This privacy is no longer 'a neutral area that will not be challenged'. Ironically, this segregation, setting children apart, has made them easier to exploit commercially and to study scientifically. Once everything is known about childhood, that is the end of childhood. Children have never been more exposed to the glare of everything. Children, like adults, are made to speak and know about everything. This violates Winnicott's central notion of *incommunicardo*, the subject's privacy and 'urgent need *not to be found*' (1963, p. 187, my italics) and of 'the primordial experience occurring in solitude' (p. 190).

We have come full circle. Winnicott and others were privilege to the inaugural moment of primary illusionment at just the time when its provision was about to disappear, not via the prophylactic way of Oedipus, which makes loss almost bearable, but via a violent excess which turns loss into rage. This real slipping away of the nuclear self, that we have described, is marked by every last-ditch stand for individuality – *my* freedoms, *my* rights, *my* pleasure, *my* sexuality – as a consolation for the end of all of these. If we take Grotstein's (1978) model of mental space, we have moved from the *three* dimensions of the Oedipal structuring to a two-dimensional loss of density (narcissistic), and may be approaching the line or the single point of maximal intensity, the zero of mental life. As Baudrillard says, we are approaching the era of 'total self-seduction', the era of 'a digital Narcissus instead of a triangular Oedipus' (1979, p. 175).

New skills, greater performance

Given that there is no going back, now that nothing traditional (i.e. stable and repressive) is recoverable or even desirable, stripped of all the old heavy repressive baggage of selfhood and communal solidarity, we must look forward to the future of relationships. One thing is already clear, everything will be skills-based. This is the global success of human-relations training, driven as it has been since the 1960s by the need for total interactivity and communicability within the large corporations. Untroubled by depth, without a constant centre or essence, we are freed up for continuous retraining and reskilling in every sphere. This reskilling will be carried out through video and IT, with less and less human involvement. Women and children are felt to be the most susceptible and willing participants.

Children brought up in more traditional settings may now be at a considerable disadvantage with their on-going propensity for stability, privacy, anxiety and a certain bondedness. They will lack the flexibility, adaptability and cool indifference demanded increasingly by the system. We can no longer expect to figure the paradoxical labyrinth of postmodernity. In fact it is uncool to try. The best of us try to learn and *use* the system, the global system. The cool thing is to use the codes, understand the new languages, to enjoy the dissonance, enjoy the carnival. Be an insider, forget the content (depth), focus on the form, the strategy, the profitability, the lifestyle options, learn to read and consume the signs. Analysis and interpretation become irrelevant and bespeak a long-gone metaphysics, a foundational view, an ontological perspective.

Consequently, it no longer makes sense to speak of *living* together in any simple, permanent or committed sense. Relation ships have become highly self-conscious, knowledge/skills/ performance-based, legalistic operations. They are the explosive centre from which all the foreclosed problems of postmodernity continuously threaten to erupt. Hence the need for intensive and proliferating skills training on techniques of involvement which maximize pleasure and eliminate pain. Sexual relationships are made to bear the brunt of the impossible clash between performance-related love, on the one hand, and the violent real of personal abjection, on the other, at a time when they are least supported by any enduring social fabric. Or, to put it another way, too much craving for love and affection is channelled into the sexual relationship at just the time in which such relationships have become most problematic in their shallowness and ephemerality. A vicious circle is set up, a kind of ultimately uninhabitable sexual ghetto is created: I *demand* you to love me (because I didn't have it as a child, and I can't get it from anywhere else). I cannot stand the intensity of your demand, not least because I have the same demands of my own that I want *you* to gratify. Fuck you if you won't love me. Yes. And fuck you too. Rejection gratifies the archaic super-ego, but also increases demand.

The legalistic frameworks and guidelines now surround all types of relationships to guard against the possibilities of abuse, harassment, discrimination, intimidation, exploitation and so on all testify to the absolute *presence* (unrepressed) of unassimilated pain. Notions of social and sexual hygiene and security pervade all contemporary life as the final paranoid denial of affect. Insurance against death, against sudden accident, against serious illness, against job-loss, protection policies, personal alarms, alarms at home, at work, in the car, all screeching and screaming at us *from the outside*. We must be secure. Our happiness depends upon security. Our communicational skills, our sexual and behavioural skills, these labours of love and perfection to close off any cracks, the intense work we have put into our own sexual and economic freedoms, have made the pain of life unbearable.

What is left are *model* relationships – relationships as image, hollowed out from the inside, as it were, while no one was noticing. Everything looks the same, but everything has gone. The missing depth dimension is matched only by the brilliance of the image. The real of relationship is replaced by fabrication and performance. The sacrament of marriage, which only thirty years ago it was considered a crime to break up, has been replaced by limited contracts and faultless pain-free separation. Without something of that depth and solitude, everything evaporates into the misery of continuous entertainment, and everything becomes unreal, in which the trick is not to feel the pain.

In David Lynch's 1986 film *Blue Velvet*, American small-town provincial life, complete with good college teenage couple, uncovers a (brutal) hidden reality of drugs and sadomasochism represented in the first instance by the shocking apparition of a severed ear in the grass – a close-up shows it to be crawling with ants. The storyline is complete when the hero rescues the woman, kills her torturer and marries his college sweetheart. What is interesting about this film is that it catches us between two images: of the wholesomely good 1950s; and the vicious but ultimately silly stereotype of a perverse drug culture. The images are juxtaposed, yet are eaten away all the while from the inside by the insects.

As Zizec says in relation to the fundamental ambiguity of the image in contemporary culture, 'it is a kind of barrier enabling the subject to maintain distance from the Real, protecting him/her against its irruption, yet its very obtrusive "hyperrealism"[9] evokes the nausea of the Real' (1992, p. 129–30).

This is what Jameson designates as our new and historically

original dilemma that involves our insertion as individual subjects into a set of radically discontinuous (imagistic) realities ranging from the still surviving spaces of bourgeois private life all the way to the unimaginable decentring of global capital itself (1991, p. 413) If those still surviving (transitional, private, solitary) spaces are shrinking fast, will there indeed come a time when no one will *remember* what they stood for?

Similarly, Lyotard (1988) speaks of late capitalism as part of a whole process of complexification, which ultimately is a process that proceeds *without us*. He emphasizes the inhumanity of the system, by which the human race is being 'pulled forward' without possessing the slightest means, he alleges, for mastering it. The electronic and information network spread over the earth's surface gives rise to a global capacity for memorizing, but he points to the paradox implied by this memory in that, in the final analysis, it is *nobody's memory*. We are now in the domain of what Lyotard calls, 'the infinite realization of the sciences, technologies and capitalism', and to the ironic production of the '*too beautiful*' (p. 122), the too well simulated, that leads to perfect closure – the exclusion of experience.

A process has accelerated in the last thirty years in which what we might call a huge negative space has opened up within what was formerly a great religious and secular tradition of *faith*. This loss of faith in the great ideologies, has led to what the Mexican poet Octavio Paz has noted as the appearance of 'the ghosts of religion': The emptiness can be filled with caricatures such as communism or fascism or total ideas, or with sects, all this flowering of superstitious selves in the Western world (1986, p. 18). Into this negative space, come animal rights, fundamental-isms, eco-terrorism, new-age philosophies and so on. These are not moral commitments in any old sense, which always allowed space for the immoral, amoral or the irreligious, but rather paranoid domains of *pure* meaning, unsullied, uncomplicated and requiring *no* personal sacrifice. These new cults increasingly threaten to mop up the free-floating moral energy generated by the entropy of capitalism in its virulent post-Marxist phase, and parallels what Baudrillard has called the more generalized 'terroristic fundamentalism of this new sacrificial religion of *performance*' (1992, pp. 106–7, my italics).

It will be to our performance that we must continuously sacrifice ourselves. Getting the very best out of people (of oneself), at work, at leisure, at sport, at sex, what we all now experience as much tougher, leaner, thinner lives, hidden from us only thinly by the promise, for the few, of economic advancement. Perform or die. What Thatcher and the New Right have done is *concentrated* the mind and removed once and for all the subversive transitional space, and replaced it with intimidation, extortion and protectionism. Everything is simplified: perform *and* die.

But there may still be hope. There are pockets of conviviality, congeniality and friendliness. Perhaps a parallel universe exists, unknown and unseen and therefore incapable of representation and degradation. This is part of the stubbornly persistent real of the social, which is paradoxically beyond and yet always present. It is the *immediacy* of the encounter, the spark, the light, the instant *before* words, and which is lost without trace as soon as we speak. It cannot form the basis of a relationship because it is totally ephemeral, but no relationship has any liveliness at all without participation in this real. Neither is it a transitional space, but it is what Winnicott sought to foster by that term and with his notion of the *incommunicardo*. Once it is named it is trapped and lost. It is not part of any mental apparatus, conscious or unconscious, and therefore it is not part of psychoanalysis, and yet any psychothera-peutic process would be dead without it. It is what is cynically evoked in commercials that use rural idylls, landscapes, etc., only to perish instantly on contact with this real. In the increasingly extreme conditions of our culture in the West, less and less of this liveliness can infuse relationships, because the *space* (free, neutral, secret, transitional) required has been colonized in *advance*. The crucial question now is whether or not this is indeed an irreversible process.

Notes

1. Here, I must beg the reader's indulgence at the outset. These assertions push events to an extreme. Normality still exists, but I

want to depict and theorize psychoanalytically about underlying disintegrative trends. These trends are often hyped in the tabloid media, they are often ignored or minimalized in contemporary discussions centring on relationships and psychotherapy. Psychotherapists, as part of their work, tend to emphasize the positive and want to be supportive. Here, at least, greater freedom is called for, indeed a certain malediction.

2. This breakdown and loss is real and is increasing. Against the criticism that this assertion is merely part of a modern moral panic and nostalgia, or so-called 'golden age-ism', we must cite, for instance, British Home Office figures that show a sevenfold increase in reported violent crime within a generation, and a massive 40 per cent, increase during the 1980s. People who live in poor areas are seven times more likely to suffer from violent crime than those in more prosperous middle-class areas. On the other hand, we are not asserting that the 1950s or any other period (the late-Victorian period for instance) was necessarily 'better' in any simplistic sense, or that there was ever any golden age to which we might return. However, the decline is no longer localized in poor or disadvantaged areas. Furthermore, *this* decline is unique as it takes place within the context of a radical moral indeterminacy.

3. Psychoanalysis makes abundantly clear that the self and its stability is not in any sense *pre*-given or automatic. The self is a *social* construct. It has to be formed within a social milieu, which involves deep, reliable and sustained contact with significant others over a long period. What happens is on the microsocial level and what is deemed essential for emotional stability is what, for instance, Bion (1967) calls 'reverie' and what Winnicott calls 'environmental provision' or 'holding' (see, for example, Winnicott, 1956).

4. This 'end' is paradoxical. Psychoanalysis is about the unconscious, but if this is exposed as our (modern) myth, if it becomes simply irrelevant or unnecessary, or if it is simply 'liberated' or overthrown, where does this leave psychoanalysis? This is where Lacan becomes important with his dogmatic assertion that the unconscious persists and insists it is a kernel of radical otherness and difference (Lacan, 1968).

5. The maternal feminine has nothing specifically to do with women or with mothers, but refers to an underlying principle of Being, beyond culture, the law, beyond anything that we might say or do. In

this reaction, Being is invoked erroneously as a consolation.

6. British headmasters report (September 1995) a threefold increase in exclusions from school in the last three years, and exclusions are now happening even at the primary level. Clearly increasing pressures on school to get results are part of this problem, but many teachers will say that they are having to deal with more and more unsocialized children, who are potentially violent and are impossible to contain in the classroom.

7. The use of the term Oedipus (Oedipal process, etc.) is not meant to be taken too literally in this context. I am using the term in its Lacanian sense, as a *structuring* phenomenon, by which *human* desire becomes possible. In this sense the term does not only refer to the modern Western nuclear family, and the two movements referred to are not necessarily carried out by a biological mother and a father.

8. This polarization is somewhat unfair. Winnicott and others (the British Independents) were of course aware that children were far from innocent. But they did privilege the innate capacity, given good enough mothering, for spontaneity, concern and creativity. They have been criticized for this emphasis on the mother (see Phillips, 1993).

9. So-called hyperrealism is the more real than real – the media *creation* of reality in a flood of imagery, in which the actual events become irrelevant, and it becomes impossible to tell the real from the fake (see, for instance, Eco, 1986).

References

Baudrillard, J, (1979), *Seduction*, Paris: Editions Galilee; translation by Brian Singer, Culture Texts, 1990
—— (1983), *Fatal Strategies*, Paris: Editions Grasset, Semiotexte/Pluto Press
—— (1990), *The Transparency of Evil*, Paris: Editions Galilee; translation by James Benedict, Verso, 1993
—— (1992), *The Illusion of the End*, Paris: Editions Galilee; translation by Chris Turner, Polity, 1994
Bettelheim, B. (1976), *The Uses of Enchantment*, Thames and Hudson
Bion, F. (ed.) (1992), *W. R. Bion Cogitations*, Karnac
Bion, W. (1967), *Second Thoughts: Selected Papers on Psychoanalysis*, Heinemann
Cooper, D. (1971), *The Death of the Family*, Allen Lane, The Penguin Press
Eco, U. (1973), *Travels in Hyperreality*, Gruppo Editoriale Fabbri-Bompani, Sonzono, Etas, S.p.A.; translation Harcourt Brace Jovanovich
Freud, S. (1914), 'On Narcissism: An Introduction', Standard Edition, 14, pp. 67–102

Grotstein, J. (1978), 'Inner Space: Its Dimensions and Its Coordinates', *International Journal of Psycho-Analysis,* 59, pp. 55–61

Jameson, F. (1991), *Postmodernism, or the Cultural Logic of Late Capitalism,* Verso

Klein, M. (1933), 'The Early Development of Conscience in the Child', *in The Writings of Melanie Klein,* Hogarth Press, 1975, pp. 248–57

Lacan, J. (1968), *Speech and Language in Psychoanalysis,* translated with notes and commentary by Antony Wilden, The Johns Hopkins University Press

Lyotard, J.-F. (1988), *The Inhuman,* Paris: Editions Galilee; Cambridge: Polity 1991

Paz, O. (1986), 'The Ghosts of Religion'?, *Listener,* Vol.115, No.2956, 17.4.86, pp. 18–20

Phillips, A. (1993), *On Kissing, Tickling and Being Bored* Faber and Faber.

Weatherill, R. (1994), *Cultural Collapse,* Free Association Books

Winnicott, D. (1951), 'Transitional Objects and Transitional Phenomena', in *Winnicott,* 1956, pp. 229–42

— (1956) *Through Paediatrics to Psychoanalysis,* Hogarth

— (1963) 'Communicating and Not Communicating Leading to a Study of Certain Opposites', in *Winnicott* l965a, pp. 179–92

— (1965), *The Maturational Processes and the Facilitating Environment,* Hogarth

— (1988), *Human Nature,* Free Association Books

Zizec, S. (1992), *Enjoy Your Symptom,* Routledge

Commentary
REFLECTING NEW MEANINGS

One of the organizing ideas of this book was that contributors would address the same general questions about their work, the society they live in and the connections between the two. They would concentrate on specific aspects of social change, agreed in advance. The style they chose to develop their chapter in was up to them. Rob Weatherill's chapter incorporates complex ideas and draws on a literature that some might find demanding. Perhaps paradoxically in the deep and challenging contribution resulting from one of Rob's points is that we are all surface now, we are untroubled by depths, all things reflect.

If these ideas and sources are unfamiliar the best advice might be to dive right in and immerse yourself in the chapter. In so doing you may find that the way he expresses his argument and the nature of that argument are tied together. There are some thoughts about the main features underlying the sorts of changes Rob is talking about in the final chapter in this book. At this point there are a number of things we can consider about how his approach links with those of the other chapters and how his argument contributes to that question about what can be done that remains our rationale in this book.

We need to think about the sort of person being described and, in particular, if it is valid to think about the meaning of their (our) lives? Then we can ask what are the possible spaces that are left for any change? But, first we are presented with a picture of our society and our changing world that is bleak in the extreme and we have to try and assimilate this. Other writers in this book have taken some of the same circumstances but have seen them as somehow less resolved, with more scope for opportunity.

Rob is not just saying that now image is important. He is going much further to argue that there is no more depth, only surfaces. The horror is that there is nothing real at all. It is as if the forces now acting on the individual are greater than at any time in the past, or if not greater then more corrosive. Given that, even if we just take the twentieth century in the West, we have had the world wars, the Holocaust and the nuclear standoff – what is so bad about now? The answer seems to be that the new age of anxiety, which so many of our contributors talk about, is accompanied by a breakdown not only of those things that allow us to enjoy relationships with others, be they intimate love or the solidarity of fellow feeling, but also of any sense of a mental life of our own. We can survive attack from outside but not from inside at the same time.

Going back to Shakespeare, we know the expression that 'all the world's a stage and all the men and women merely players'. Getting real has never been easy. We have always been seduced by images and of course there have always been pain and despair. There have also always been inequality, oppression, injustice and want. But we must resist a too easy assumption about social determinism, about the relationship between despair and circumstance. We have probably all encountered people who have thrived despite adversity, dreadful upbringings or traumatic events.[1] Rob seems to be saying that, even if we survive, all we have to face is a time of total restlessness and irritability and that we are on the edge of a fatal futility. Getting real, at least in the sense that we have understood this in the past, is no longer an option.

While writing these comments, and listening to a classical music station on the radio, two advertisements were broadcast. The first was for the very successful *Hello!* magazine and trailed three stories: a supermodel jetting out of the country with her personal trainer, the gold taps in a 'star's' bathroom and the 'fairy tale' preparation for a society wedding. Immediately after was a Salvation Army advert as part of their 'Red Shield Appeal' to provide shelter for the homeless of our cities. Such commonplace juxtapositions leave no room for irony. One radio commentator has recently described *Hello!* magazine as exemplifying the banality of fame which has taken over from the banality of evil as the defining motif of our times. Political theorist and philosopher Hannah Arendt (1963) used the expression 'the banality of evil' in describing leading Nazi Eichmann at his trial in Jerusalem. She was concerned to show how extremely average people could become instruments and executioners of monstrous design. The American writer of what he calls 'memory books' but his reviewers call oral history, Studs Terkel, argues that Arendt's analysis can be supplemented with a recognition of the 'evil of banality': 'Trivia is a joke, fine. But not when it chokes you; when there is no difference between politics, news and entertainment.' Terkel is fighting against the demise of history, the development of what he calls collective Alzheimer's disease: 'Without history there is no lasting present.'[2] If the ways Arendt's insights have been developed rings true for you then perhaps Rob's vision seems more than apt.

The people inhabiting the world he describes might be freed from old repressive taboos but they live with increased levels of anxiety. Looking at young people today it is possible to see this clash played out. On the one hand, young people appear more streetwise, more knowing, more sophisticated. Yet they have less access to the world than children in the past. We might call their worldliness a 'virtual' one. They may have computers and TV channels but they are not allowed to walk to school alone or play in the park. There has always been the tragedy of children being murdered by strangers and it is doubtful if the number has gone up. But the perception is that the world is more dangerous and it is perception that structures the life experience of the children. In a piece in the *Guardian* (6 January 1996) Linda Grant identified how each abduction and murder takes a little more freedom from children. The names of the murderers or the places they murdered in become bricks in the wall that imprisons children. The 'prison' the children end up in is the home. Here they have to live with what ought to be the concerns of adults: drugs, violence, the problems of marital break-up. They do so via access to a therapeutic language, a language gleaned from TV soap operas. This offers them a script for trauma, an approved set of reactions. For example, they will have seen divorce played out many times and will have learned the appropriate verbal reactions. But these don't reflect their feelings, they are upset by the event and by the disparity between what they feel and what they think they should express. These resulting hollow responses are one manifestation of the 'surfaces'.[3]

The picture discussed in this chapter is a grim one, perhaps deservedly. Can we no longer speak of living together in any simple, permanent or committed sense? Is there some hope, a spark of immediacy before words? The task is to find new meanings. This might seem a very small thing to take consolation in, and it certainly represents less of an opportunity for change than that seen by many of our contributors.

Vaclav Havel talks of hope being a state of mind not a state of the world and many writers in the past have shared a recognition of what Wordsworth called the 'inherent and indestructible qualities of the human mind'.[4] But the space to develop that state of mind and to exercise any indestructible quality has been eroded. The force and poetry of our cultural language have been increasingly thinned down. If we insist on talking of the beauty of, say, air fresheners or the tragedy of dandruff then what words can we use when we really want to express something profound. We need to be able to communicate face to face in such a way as to preserve such contacts from the instrumental way we exist publicly, where how we can use someone, or how we can prevent someone being used, is dominant.[5]

Down in the wreckage with Rob the immediacy of the encounter – the instant before words offers the opportunity to start with re-creating something intimate before moving on to the social. At least psychotherapists have experience of operating in this area. What is needed then is not a social project but the authenticity of my encounter with you. There is something about the small scale, it is invoked at various points – Bob Hinshelwood on the 'creative impulse' for example – that is becoming central in this book.

Don't think our contributors are saying we have to just live in intimate spaces. The scale of the world and the scope of our social contacts will not go away, we can't change that. But it is this level that offers the chance of a new blueprint, not the blueprints we have been offered in the past. Grand schemes, rules, ideologies have not worked. Work has changed, public space has changed, a sense of certainly about who we are and what we should be doing has changed. Perhaps it is a good thing. In *King Lear*, blind and despairing Gloucester thinks he has thrown himself from the cliffs. Still living he resolves, 'Henceforth I'll bear affliction till it do cry out itself "Enough, enough" and die.' The contemplation of horror, or the confrontation of despair, can generate resolve. This chapter has us approaching a zero of mental life. Perhaps this can be a spur to living together differently.

Notes

1. Michael Rutter (1979) identified some children who even with the most terrible homes and the most stressful experiences seem to come through unscathed and show stable, healthy, personality development. He called these children the 'invulnerables'.

2. Studs Terkel's book about growing old in America is called *Coming of Age*. He was interviewed about it in the *Observer* on 28 May 1995.

3. Many of these same concerns are explored in a detailed academic study by Rutter and Smith (1995). They identify individualism, isolation and stress both to not fail and to not be at odds with prevalent peer-group culture as most important in the 'explosion of social and psychological problems in the young'.

4. Vaclav Havel is quoted in Seamus Heaney, *The Redress of Poetry*, Faber and Faber.

5. This is the subject area of psychoanalyst Jacques Lacan and critical theorist Jurgen Habermas, who approach both understanding and acting in very different ways. See, for an introduction, albeit not an easy one, into the work of these two writers, Sullivan (1986) and Habermas (1984).

References

Arendt, H. (1963), *Eichmann in Jerusalem. A Report on the Banality of Evil*. Faber and Faber

Habermas, J. (1984), *The Theory of Communicative Action*. Beacon Press

Rutter, M. (1979), Maternal Deprivation 1972–1978: New Findings, New Concepts, New Approaches, *Child Development*

Rutter, M. & Smith, D. J. (1995), *Psychological Disorders in Young People,* John Wiley and Sons

Sullivan, E. Ragland, (1986), *Jacques Lacan and the Philosophy of Psychoanalysis,* University of Illinois Press

Chapter 5
POPULAR CULTURE
Barry Richards

This chapter seeks to use some insights from the field of psychodynamic inquiry in developing our understanding of contemporary politics and of popular participation in the political process. It links some conceptualizations of the present 'postmodern' and 'anti-political' age with a psychoanalytical approach to understanding individuals' relationships to the political domain.

I was asked to approach the book's three basic questions through a consideration of popular culture. This yields abundant material with which to tackle the questions of what it is like to live in contemporary Britain, of what recent social changes there have been and how they have affected us, and of what reforms we might propose to make it a better society.

Popular culture and psychic development

The history of popular mass culture in a society like Britain is a long and complex one, going back over two hundred years to the origins of modern consumer society. However, as an oversimplified but useful starting point we can suggest that in the second half of this century the power of popular culture to reach deeply into personal experience and to enter the foundations of personal identity was significantly enhanced by a number of developments, particularly the emergence of television and of what came to be known as youth culture, or subcultures, based around the consumption of pop music and fashion. A whole academic discipline – cultural studies – has emerged partly around the recognition of the importance of these and related developments, and it is not possible here to engage with the vast amount of commentary, theory and research which that has involved. I will offer instead a psychoanalytically coloured account of what post-war popular culture has meant for psychic development.

It was until recently an accepted wisdom in many circles, especially among the left-liberal intelligentsia, from which psychotherapists tend to be drawn, that the impact of popular culture was on balance a negative one, especially in so far as television and the growth of many forms of mass leisure were concerned. Everyone will be familiar with the terms of this critique: popular culture is equated with the resort to the lowest common denominator, the manipulation of passive consumers, the exploitation of a gullible public, the flooding of society with goods and images which are cheap, superficial, sentimental, tacky, etc. There have been many psychoanalytic theorizations of this critique, in terms of the neurotic anxieties, the defences, the psychic impoverishment and narcissistic traits which popular cultural forms have been seen to embody.

In keeping with the spirit of much work in cultural studies, I want to advance a more positive psychoanalytic account. This would see cultural forms such as sport and pop music, and our relationships with some of the material commodities and imagery of the consumer society, as providing at least some possibilities for psychic integration. The psychoanalytic test of a good cultural form, on this view, is whether it provides us with an opportunity for some expression of primitive or libidinal need, as well as providing an experience of reality and limits, and of some form of containing authority. Through experiencing the tensions between such forces, and the enhancement through that experience of benign relationships with authority, our own individual capacities for containing ourselves are developed. This is a familiar model of early psychic development; one implication of it is that the capacity to experience one's own needs while also coming to accept reality and be contained by it is never finally achieved, and needs to be rehearsed and confirmed constantly throughout adult life.

Let us take one illustrative example of this. Sport is an increasingly popular pursuit, I would argue, because it provides intense experiences of both bodily pleasure and of rule-based social authority, with the latter ultimately in the ascendant. However, the rules of sport are not vested in the state or any other organ of traditional authority. While the governing bodies of particular sports may be grounded in social élites, and in many respects act in conservative ways, they are not part of a system of ideologically dominant institutions. The rules of the sport can usually be changed in response to the needs of players or spectators. Sport is thus a paradigmatic institution of modern popular culture, as well as an ancient constituent of many human societies. The increasing importance of commercial considerations in the organization of many sports complicates but does not vitiate this analysis.

Changing modes of containment

In a previous work (Richards, 1994), I develop this argument around a case study of football. There are also other case studies in the book, all oriented towards an appreciative psychoanalytic approach to popular culture, but here I want to make another general point. This is that the increasing prominence, over the last fifty years, of popular cultural forms is a cultural change of great significance, for it means that the external supports for internal capacities for containment are increasingly to be found in those cultural forms, rather than in the institutions and practices associated with traditional forms of authority. These traditional forms would include the churches, the authority vested in hierarchical relationships associated with the workplace, the respect accorded to professionals and to scientific knowledge, and the general structures of deference associated with a highly stratified social order.

It was one of the founding insights of sociology in the nineteenth century that the authority of religion was declining. Yet a common-sense sociology today might still assume that if we try to locate the main sources of authority in today's social landscape we would find them in the traditional restraints of religion and in other easily recognizable forms of social authority: the expert, the boss, the police, the government, the civil service and so on. In psychoanalytic terms this is in a sense an attempt to map the super-ego on to social institutions, and is one which finds it in those institutions which seem most explicitly designed to carry super-ego functions. But at the same time many everyday observations, coming together into another brand of common sense, testify to the waning capacity of these authorities to mesh effectively with individuals' super-egos. We know that the unquestioned credibility of all experts and professionals is a thing of the past, that many workplaces have 'flat' hierarchies, that distrust of the police is widespread and so on. We know that although some religions are as strong, globally, as ever, and have an increasing presence in Britain, our national culture in Britain can never again be bound to any theologically based moral code.

While politicians and political institutions have, perhaps, never enjoyed much moral authority, they have none the less in the past been able to share in the command of that part of super-ego territory held automatically by all and any élite groups in British society. Now, however, as that élite has fragmented, and politicians are exposed to contemptuous interrogation on television and to regular scandals, they have to compete without advantage against astrologers, counsellors, talk-show hosts and all comers as they struggle to lay claim to some form of credible authority, to some affinity with the national super-ego.

The institution of the family occupies a complex place in this picture of cultural change. In terms of individual psychic development, the family must remain the crucible of super-ego formation. It was the argument of Christopher Lasch and others that the weakening of the family as a morally confident and instructive force is at the heart of modern *malaise*. A strong but well-integrated super-ego is seen as the basis of healthy ego development, and the argument was that the contemporary demoralized family could not provide this. Again much everyday evidence may seem to confirm this: it points to a change whereby specific codes are not transmitted across the generations as may once have been the case, and offspring are freeing themselves more and more in adolescence or early adulthood from specific restraints which their parents may have enjoined upon them. Indeed, we have for some years been able to see the second phase of this change, in which many parents have largely withdrawn from the task of transmitting specific prescriptive codes, at least in relation to some aspects of sexuality, and to aesthetic and other cultural values.

Yet this cultural change may not necessarily testify to a corrosion of the fundamental socializing power of the family, and of its ability to establish moral capacities in the individual. The bonds between parents and children are not weakening in intensity, though they are becoming more complex and unpredictable in their effects. If anything, the experience of these bonds is becoming more intense, as the belief that family is destiny, in an emotional sense, gains wider acceptance. Perhaps the main legacy of psychoanalysis to popular culture to date is in the spread of this belief, though it may have a number of other sources. An appreciation of the ways in which parenting and early relationships leave indelible marks on the psyche, and an urge to explore and unpack those relationships, whether in anger or gratitude, are features of the 'therapeutic culture' in which, arguably, we now live.

So while the family is no longer the centrepiece in an ensemble of institutions of authority which functioned coherently together to secure the transmission of specific moral precepts, it none the less still produces individuals with very strong moral capacities. Indeed, on the psychoanalytic view that the origins of morality are in nurture, it is hard to see how the family could not retain this function. Yet these capacities are also established through the child's involvement in the wider social world. This was always the case, but as that social world has changed so have the modes of its contribution to psychic life. Rather than acting broadly in concert with familial authority (whatever strains and contradictions there might have been within and between traditional authorities), the social world is now a variegated field of pressures and possibilities. Moral capacities and principles endowed by the family, while still very strong, are given content, negotiated and elaborated in the individual's on-going interactions with social institutions and cultural practices. And as the spheres of consumption, leisure and entertainment have expanded, and taken a prominent place in those interactions, the institutions and practices which can offer support to the moral organization of the psyche are increasingly part of what we might call popular culture. Of course the role of schools and other educational institutions remains large in the development of character and in the landscape of the national culture. However, with the weakening of many social boundaries these institutions to some extent no longer represent independent or separate spheres of value but are conduits for the circulation of values (e.g. ideas about the importance of expressive individual self-development) which are present in many informal spheres of popular culture.

From the standpoint of the left-liberal critique referred to above, now that the market and the alleged illusions or untruths of consumer society have replaced the old once-respected institutions of authority as the major forces in contemporary culture, there is a moral vacuum. The market is amoral in its basic principles, and as market relations become dominant everywhere so morality shrivels. While this may still be a necessary and fruitful analysis, it is not adequate as a statement of the most significant trends. In particular it is not adequate, nor even to a large degree accurate, to see popular culture as embodying moral vacuity. One has to think only of the content of most television 'soaps' to appreciate this point.

Televisual culture and therapeutic culture

The appeal of the soap may be attributed to its embodying the convergence of two very powerful forms of contemporary culture. One, obviously, is what we might call 'televisual culture': the organization of leisure time and family life around the television, the importance to many people of the content of television programmes, and the interrelationships between television and other areas of leisure such as sport and music. This notion of televisual culture is a very crude one, but serves here to indicate the importance of this particular technological form which enables an endless variety of dramatized human situations to be experienced in every home. Many of the dramatic situations most commonly used during the relatively brief history of television, such as the Western, the detective story and the soap, can clearly be recognized as reflecting preoccupations with moral issues, in the broad sense of focusing on what people do to each other and on the importance of trying to distinguish right from wrong. (In some of the more sophisticated soaps and dramas, a central message may be the difficulty of doing the latter.)

All the soaps are very largely taken up with dramatizations of moral issues: how people relate to each other, what choices they make, how they respond to the misfortunes and burdens life puts upon them, what consequences follow from their actions and so on. They are rarely concerned with questions of political values, and even in their chosen domain of interpersonal values they are not usually prescriptive in the sense of advocating absolute principles. They are none the less didactic in their insistence that our conduct in relationships and in the discharge of our responsibilities is a complex matter which is, or ought to be, of central concern to all of us.

This indicates the connection with the second contemporary phenomenon, referred to already as 'therapeutic culture'. By this we mean the growth (over the last thirty years or so) of interest in emotional life, and of tendencies to self-reflection. While the most obvious representatives of this are the multitude of psychotherapies and counselling practices which have developed in the last fifteen years or so, this cultural trend is also embodied in many other ways: in the proliferation of agony columns and help lines, in trends in management theory and practice and in educational theory and practice, in characters found in films and books and so on – including, importantly, in the content of television programmes such as the soaps. These carry 'therapeutic' values in their preoccupation with character and their implicit messages that relationships are all-important and feelings matter.

In making this link between, as it were, *Brookside* and the British Association of Counselling (or, more distantly, between the less 'therapeutically' focused *Coronation Street* and the distinctly unpopulist Institute of Psychoanalysis), I am suggesting that the psychotherapies are part of a broad cultural trend. Moreover, they play a key generative role in that trend, in that psychotherapy, especially in its more intensive forms, is a kind of frontier or vanguard in the search for deeper and more satisfying forms of self-reflection and emotional understanding, and for better ways of interpersonal relating. Psychotherapy is perhaps the strongest example of the belief that a (reflective) focus on feelings can be productive of changes in identity. Pursuing this line of argument, we could say that psychotherapy is a major force in giving stimulus and shape to the contemporary preoccupations with feeling, subjectivity and identity, and to the hopes that feelings can be understood and identities changed, if not easily. The sociologist Paul Halmos (1965) offered a prescient formulation of this phenomenon in his account of the counselling 'faith' at an early stage of its development in Britain.

The growth of this 'reflexivity', as these preoccupations have been called, has been a topic of much interest to some sociologists in recent years (see in particular the more recent work of Anthony Giddens, e.g. 1992). It has been linked to changes in gender roles, and seen as part of a general trend towards democratization, in so far as it is linked to a wish for greater self-determination, universalistic personal autonomy and freedom from the constraints of traditional expectations and from other burdens of the past.

The expanding world of the psychotherapies and counselling

practices can contribute strongly to our understandings of social changes, through the insights into emotional needs and dilemmas which these practices can generate. However, they are also very much a part of those changes. Indeed, I have been suggesting that they are an emblematic and core factor in the emergence of the 'therapeutic culture' of our day. The therapeutic, self-reflexive impulse has spread from the consulting room and its other points of origin, and entered popular culture at many levels and in many areas. A morally toned concern with feelings is an intrinsic part of popular culture.

The upbeat assessment of therapeutic culture presented above must of course be set against a number of more negative ones. In these debates, a lot may hang on the specific kinds of therapy being discussed, though all psychotherapists have some responsibility to consider questions about the wider effects and affinities of their professional practice, and cannot assume that these are uncomplicatedly benign. There is a view of therapeutic culture which sees the turn to therapy as symptomatic of, and reinforcing, a *malaise* of narcissistic emptiness. There is another which argues that the impact of psychotherapy, perhaps especially in its more psychoanalytic forms, is amoral, in the dissolving effect that analysis may have on any moral code based on defensive identifications with others. The psychological basis of commitment to dogmatic ideology, especially when this is associated with the readiness to hurt and kill others, can easily be seen in this way as a defence, but it is hard to stop the analysis there: on a psychoanalytic view there is at least a component of safety-seeking or some other defensive need in any attachment to social values.

This revelation lies at the heart of Philip Rieff's (1966) profound exploration of the implications of Freudian thought. Rieff's post-Freudian 'psychological man' is free of neurotic commitments to collective causes, being a more self-possessed person who – following Freud's own (1921) analysis of the group as a form of illness – mistrusts any invitation to join the chorus. Rieff himself is deeply ambivalent about this development, since he also tends to see the new personality-type as at risk of being superficial and empty. But his work does not engage with the more recent and positive assessments of contemporary identities.

Psychic development in postmodern culture

There are other ways, beyond therapeutic culture, in which we should see popular culture as offering opportunities for the elaboration and consolidation of moral capacities. In classical psychoanalytic language, this means opportunities for confirming the integration of super-ego functions into the ego; in a post-Freudian language, we may instead talk of external supports for internal capacities for containment. The provision of these supports has passed from traditional sources of authority to a wider and constantly changing array of institutional and cultural forms, and so the modes of moral regulation are changing. Popular culture has now quite extensively become a field of value, of moral discovery and affirmation. While this has always been true for some of its forms, such as sport, it is now increasingly true of other parts of it where we have not expected to find such dimensions. In the consumption of consumer goods and the creation of imagery, for example, questions of ethical value are increasingly involved (most obviously concerning the environment), both in consumer decisions and in commercial strategies. While these are complex developments, around some of which a measure of cynicism may be healthily retained, the increasing interpenetration of entertainment and charity, and of commerce and concern, marks a reconstitution of the commercial dimension of the 'popular', a weakening within it of purely libidinal or selfish elements and a strengthening of reparative ones.

Alongside this development, and linked to it, there is the increasingly powerful hold of popular cultural experience on the formation of identity. For many people reared in late capitalism, our experiences of the world and of ourselves have been heavily influenced by the existence of the subcultural identities which have been multiplying. Popular culture is no longer an homogeneous trough of pleasurable experience into which working people can jump to gain temporary release from the rigours of wage labour. Though it undoubtedly continues to serve important functions of release and counterpoint to the world of work, it is now more a highly differentiated array of experiences in the choice between which, and in the consumption of which, we create important definitions of ourselves. The release it offers is often from intergenerational tensions, as in the fields of music and fashion, yet the identities to be forged are not simple ones of age, or class, but shifting combinations of those factors and of gender, ethnicity, region and many other cultural divisions. So while our need to find containment and identity in the field of popular culture is all the greater, given the fading of those social forces which used to meet our basic psychic needs for authority, the identities on offer are bewilderingly profuse, and more work is needed from the individual to make them cohere and fit.

Those familiar with the current state of social and cultural theory will recognize in the foregoing a rendering of 'postmodern' society and its characteristics of fragmentation and uncertainty. I am seeking to qualify that picture with the claim that containment is not lacking in the postmodern world (though many commentators have assumed it must be), but is differently woven into the cultural fabric. It is sought and found through participation in popular culture rather than through subjection to traditional authorities. Especially as that culture diversifies, it is consequently patterned for individuals in different ways, unlike the more homogeneous imprint of traditional moral codes. The familial endowment of moral feeling does not now mesh firmly and easily with a waiting codification; there are spaces and irregularities, a much more complex interface between early experience and social possibility, and a much greater contingency is at work in the emergence of the adult individual.

According to Rieff, psychoanalysis is at least partly responsible for the disengagement of contemporary identities from traditional politico-moral allegiances. Similarly, the psycho-therapeutic culture as a whole may be seen as a cause rather than an effect of this disengagement. Whether or not these causal hypotheses are accepted, psychoanalysis does suggest that if people in a country such as Britain are now largely free of such commitments, and not easily driven into them, then this may well be an advance. If they are more comfortably embedded in the pleasures and pluralities of the 'postmodern', they may be more sanely so. This is not to say that there is no longer any possibility of moral communities. The earlier reference to the emergence of moral communities of consumption, as an awareness of the responsibilities of consumers becomes more widespread, gives one example of a growing moralization of the public sphere. The question is rather one of what kinds of claims these communities make on their individual members, and what kind of claims they make to embodying some ideological absolutes.

Revivalist tendencies

The social and psychic forms of the new developments look different from the self-consciously totalizing movements of socialism which have been the main vehicles of hope and understanding for so many people this century. Typically these movements have been based on organizations with intellectual and moral agendas which professed completeness. In contemporary developments, stemming from 'single issue' and 'identity' politics, the omniscience often characteristic of such movements is lacking, as is the claim made on the whole of the individual who wished to support the movement or be involved in politics.

Yet beliefs in the revivability of the moral communities of old persist widely. The turn to psychoanalysis by some intellectuals of the Left in the 1980s was in the hope that it would be a source of new ways to articulate moral and political truths, and so to help revive those communities by reformulating their appeals. This hope was encouraged by the strongly moral address of some of the varieties of psychoanalytic thinking which were taken up, such as the Kleinian tradition and object-relations theory.

This theoretical turn was prompted in no small part by the electoral success of Thatcherism, which seemed to demonstrate that – in contrast to what was seen as the soulless technocratic social-democracy of the 1960s and 1970s – a galvanizing moral vision was an instrumental as well as a spiritual necessity for the dispirited Left. Thatcher, it was felt, had moved into and filled a moral vacuum left by the collapse of 1960s radicalisms, and it was concluded that this demonstrated the hunger of the electorate, and the enduring need of the people, for membership of a moral community. Acquiring an appealing 'vision thing' was therefore an imperative for the Left.

Alongside this diagnosis, it must be said, was another which took a different view. The 1980s were seen by some not primarily as a period of revived moralism, but on the contrary as one in which the public sphere, the locus of collective moralization, went into a process of serious decline. The growth of private sectors in the health and education fields, increasing pressures on public-sector services, the expansion of advertising and the commercial media, the growing influence of the tabloid press, and specific factors such as the failures of the 1984 miners' strike and of the Greenham Common encampment to achieve their ends, all contributed to a sense that far from undergoing a moral revival, however dubious the morality, Britain as a whole had sunk into a demoralized state in which people concentrated regressively on their private interests as consumers and family members because they had lost faith in the public sphere of democratic process and political morality. The prescription derived from this second diagnosis was, however, the same in essence as that derived from the first. While the first diagnosis suggested the need for a transformation of political morality, the second prescribed a programmatic resurrection of community. Both demanded a new infusion of totalizing values, acknowledging perhaps the new diversities apparent in British society but aiming none the less at an encompassing remoralization.

Psychosocial narratives

One feature of such approaches is the incorporation of a traditional brand of common sense which says 'politics not personalities', 'issues not individuals', etc. A degradation of political discourse is seen as the inevitable consequence or corollary of the rise of the 'personality cult', of increasing attention paid to the personal characteristics and circumstances of those active in political life. The moral revival of the political domain is seen from this viewpoint to require the rolling back of media practices and audience responses which inappropriately import modes of judgement from the domain of personal relationships and interpersonal attractions into the political sphere. The belief that an ever greater role is being acquired by 'spin doctors', individuals within the political parties with special responsibility for media presentation, is part of the general perception that the values that really matter have got lost. 'Soundbites', the sartorial grooming of erstwhile unkempt or inelegant politicians, the pursuit of photo opportunities and other presentational objectives are focused on and vilified, on the assumption that attention to such matters is incompatible with value-driven politics. The development of the Labour Party in recent years, and the alleged ascendancy within it of the 'beautiful people' supporters of the current leader, Tony Blair (though the trend in this direction is regarded as having begun with the previous leader but one, Neil Kinnock), is the most-quoted example of this much-bewailed phenomenon.

Yet the movement towards the personalized dramatization of politics seems inexorable. And if we are using a psychodynamic frame of reference, we should not be surprised by this, nor be inclined to regret it as the corruption of politics. The emphasis on the presentation of persons is a recognition of the importance of the leader element in group functioning, which is axiomatic in the psychoanalytic understanding of groups. The fact that leaders excite powerful feelings in a group can neither be deplored nor seized upon as a new possibility for manipulation.

It has ever been thus, though not in an unchanging way. The relationship of professional politics to the rest of society, and also the processes within that specialized domain itself, are of course changing as part of overall cultural change. They are being transformed particularly by the rise to dominance of the two aspects of contemporary culture discussed earlier, televisual culture and therapeutic culture. These two developments come together as much in representations of electoral choices, and in the political process more widely, as they do in the 'soap'.

The development of television has famously contributed to a change in political culture, especially by offering new possibilities for deployment of the 'personalities' involved. The combination of these possibilities with the rise of therapeutic culture, the growth of self-reflection and of interests in emotional life, has resulted in a complex situation which can be assessed in different ways. For the present purpose, the main point is that public appreciation of the personal qualities of leaders is now embedded in a tendency to scrutinize the personal and emotional dimensions of everything.

While the leaders' 'personalities' have always been important, we might suggest that in postmodern political culture the dominant representations of these personalities are

(a) more volatile, as part of the greater general fluidity of everything, and the vulnerability of everyone to de-idealizing forces, whether these come in tabloid feet-of-clay-exposing or therapeutic mature-disillusioning form; and

(b) more sophisticated, as a consequence of real gains in emotional reflexivity in the general culture; and

(c) more catalytic of changes in the political landscape. While 'real' political issues may be of no lesser ultimate importance, the immediacy now with which people turn to the subjective and the personal, and the connections made at deeper levels between these dimensions and the traditional political ones, mean that the impact of the 'personality' can interact much more quickly and powerfully with the impersonal agendas.

Some recent Canadian research by Stephen Kline (1996) distinguished between three factors influencing voters: ideology (values, what kind of society people believe to be best, etc.), utility (what impact voters perceive policies will have on them personally) and social narrative. The last of these refers to pictures of what kind of people the candidates are, which voters build up over time through their experiences of the candidates. Print media play a part here, but the key experiences will be of candidates on television, interacting with others – in public settings, in interviews and debates, etc. Kline found (in a study of a Canadian provincial election) that this third factor was actually the most important.

Following this line of argument, we must conclude that the kinds of 'social narrative' being constructed, or which could be constructed, around party political leaders are of considerable relevance to electoral prospects. These social narratives are perhaps best thought of as 'psychosocial' ones; they are of the kind elaborated in soaps and other television drama, in much popular literature and elsewhere. They are about the impact people have on others, the kinds of relationships they form, how they can be trusted, how much they understand of life, what parts of their characters emerge under stress, what they are trying to get for themselves, what capacities they have for generosity, forgiveness and fortitude, who and what matters to them, how hard they work, and so on (in short, what specimens of 'human nature' they are).

This is not a capitulation to 'spin-doctor' values, whatever they might be, but a recognition that 'personality' is in a sense embedded values (including political values). We might invert an insight from the 1960s and say that 'the political is personal'.

Clearly, one practical recommendation to emerge from this would be that the 'personalized social narrative' as an unavoidable dimension of politics needs careful attention. However, giving thought to it, being aware of its importance, and seeking to influence the construction of these narratives wherever possible cannot amount to a total engineering of the narrative identity of the party and its leaders. Research into political audiences and consumer markets constantly shows that publics have inexhaustible reserves of cynicism and detachment, and endless capacities for generating readings of publicity images which are hostile or tangential to those intended by the publicists.

Total image control is therefore chimerical, but 'personalities', or personalized social narratives, are very important (in 'real' as well as 'instrumental' ways). They really matter, and are not just a means of winning or losing elections. Some promotional management of these narratives is unavoidable in the competitive market, loosely speaking, of electoral politics – in party political broadcasts, in a party's general dealings with the media, and in a more diffuse way – in its internal life, which is where these narratives become fused with 'real' politics.

A similar trend can be observed in recent developments in consumer product advertising. We find there a strong move towards rhetorical styles which are not 'about' the product in any simple informative sense, but which try to embed the brand in some narrative context. The intention is that the brand, by being absorbed into human drama and human characters, will itself both absorb the qualities of these characters – whatever specific ones may be portrayed (charisma, caring, etc.) – and also take on the general quality of belonging in everyday life.

The question is not whether a personality 'cult' should develop around a leadership, but how it develops and whether it can be steered in the most advantageous way – to the enhancement, that is, of the overall political culture as well as to the advantage of the individual leader or party. Such enhancement may be gained when the narrative modelling of politics gives greater prominence and esteem to mature features of personal identity, with those features which presently are often occluded, such as the capacity to tolerate doubt and to admit error, having as much currency as the more conventionally heroic qualities such as the capacity to make tough decisions, and to stick to principles.

While it may be reasonable for some people to hold specific responsibility for this permanent dimension of a party's strategy, the issues involved should be the concern of many party activists, as they are of most voters, not the exclusive preoccupation of some specialist advisers. While we are yet some way from this, recent developments in British party politics suggest that the narrative dimension of political persuasion is now in its way quite firmly installed, albeit in some tension with an older vision of community for which these psychosocial narratives are a malign intrusion.

The anti-political age

This, however, is only a part of the radical transformation of the political sphere which is being wrought by postmodern, televisual, therapeutic culture. The shift which has been traced and advocated here, from the search for binding communities to a more low-key, complex conception of political collectivities, is required by the fact that we are now in, as Geoff Mulgan (1994) has described it, an 'anti-political age'. The disengagement of the public from electoral politics is by no means complete; elections continue to fascinate a good many people, though many of them may be sceptical none the less about what is ultimately at stake. But it is extensive, and is part of a wider and deeper phenomenon. Mulgan describes how the traditional domain of modern politics has in recent decades been increasingly unable to provide expression for a growing agenda. The new social movements have sought to extend the boundaries of the political, while even more fundamentally an agenda best thought of as 'cultural' has come for many to have the urgency and passion once commanded by politics, and to deal with some of the social questions of opportunity, satisfaction and justice which once might have been thought to be the business of 'politics' to resolve.

These changes are related to but separable from the rise of 'personalities' in politics; when the 'spin doctors' take to political strategy, they may come up with relatively conventional programmes which show little understanding of the developments Mulgan describes, such as the decline of the nation and with it the national political stage as the place where the key dramas of society are enacted, and the rise of 'identity politics', with increasing importance attached to areas of everyday life beyond the reach of conventional party politics.

With its particular sensitivities to the ties which link individuals to their communities, socio-psychodynamic thinking can contribute to the understanding of how such developments call for new forms of collectivity and community. While leaders and charisma will always count for much, the explicit context for their influence is now more psychological than ideological. While the televisual and therapeutic aspects of culture do not in themselves bring a better political culture, they certainly bring a different one. Recognition of that difference is a precondition for turning it to advantage in the creation of new forms of community, in which conceptions of belonging, of right and of duty are mediated through our new understandings of the personal and its importance.

Acknowledgement

Some of the ideas put forward in this chapter were first drafted for the 'Human Nature' study group, and developed in discussion with members of that group, which has met since February 1994 to explore psychoanalytic understanding of politics. I am grateful to members of this group, and to Nicky Gavron, its convenor, for the experience of their very productive discussions.

References

Freud, S. (1921), *Group Psychology and the Analysis of the Ego*

Giddens, A. (1992), *The Transformation of Intimacy*, Polity

Halmos, P. (1965), *The Faith of the Counsellors*, Constable

Kline, S. (1996), 'Negative Political Advertising, in M. Nava *et al.* (eds.), *Buy This Book: Current Explorations in Advertising and Consumption*, Routledge

Mulgan, G. (1994), *Politics in an Anti-political Age*, Polity

Richards, B. (1994), *Disciplines of Delight: The Psychoanalysis of Popular Culture*, Free Association Books

Rieff, P. (1966), *The Triumph of the Therapeutic*, Penguin, 1973

Commentary
SOAP OPERA, FOOTBALL AND 'SOFT' POLITICS

In British TV dramatist Dennis Potter's final work, *Cold Lazarus*, a person from the year AD 2370, seeing an image of a football crowd in late twentieth-century Britain, is amazed most of all by how close people are to each other. 'They must have been almost touching each other,' she exclaims. Potter's vision is of a future in which the *frisson* generated when people gather together is what is most feared. Despite these huge crowds at football some people argue that we are already well on the way to being a nation of watchers rather than joiners. We are also, perhaps, people well informed about a myriad of events and opinions throughout the world but not engaged in any active way with them. It is the television that is most easily seen as as the route to this passive knowledgeability. Further, or so the argument goes, television or at least an 'over-indulgence' in television impoverishes the relationship between the individual and the community he or she lives in, it detracts from active citizenship. (Over-indulgence simply means those people who watch more than you do.)

So we have on the one hand a cultural phenomenon that depends on large numbers of people at the same place at the same time – football – and on the other the TV that facilitates and epitomizes the rapid and decisive retreat into privacy. There is a juxtaposition of the two cultural forms when we see the mass development of people watching football on TV in public, mostly in pubs, and when we consider that the timing, the presentation and to some extent the spectacle of football are increasingly shaped by television.

Barry Richards's chapter gets to grips with a

relationship between popular cultural forms and the individual's psychic world. He is presenting a picture that sees, in our choices of popular cultural experience, ways we create important definitions of ourselves. In so doing he is asking us to think more positively about encounters with popular culture. He is also posing a challenge to those who too easily equate all apparent weakening of established patterns of authority with a sense of weakened containment for the individual or a decline in moral guidance in society.

In the stance he takes, Barry is recognizing a shift from certainties into complexity and unpredictability, an approach very much at one with the other contributors to this book. Where he moves apart is in his assessment of the implications of this shift. A number of our chapters look at how the individual can respond to the anxiety generated by not knowing where we stand. They look at how more intimate spaces can be shaped within which the individual can live – Rob Weatherill's chapter, for example. Barry continues to engage with the 'bewilderingly profuse' postmodern world but he sees potentials within it for release both from intergenerational tensions and traditional authorities. He takes issue with those who see the weakening of the family as a morally confident and instructive force as being at the heart of the modern *malaise*. Is it not that we have a *change* rather than a *weakening* in the intensity of the bonds?

Barry sees the growth of the therapeutic culture and the sense that the 'family is destiny' as the main gift of psychoanalysis to popular culture. This growth in interest in our emotional life (including the propensity for self-reflection) is represented in popular culture by TV soap operas. So too, is a preoccupation with moral issues, on what people do to each other and on the importance of trying to distinguish right from wrong. Soaps say that relationships are all-important and that feelings matter. Barry argues that this morally toned concern is an inherent part of popular culture.

Not only does popular culture speak to the way we seek to define ourselves and the way we engage with moral issues but, through sport, it also offers us a way of engaging with rule-based social authority. This begins in childhood games where there is a serious engagement with rules and procedures and it is this that often appears to be the real rationale, or at least the main reason for the game carrying on. In his chapter, Barry does not talk a great deal about sport (he does refer to other work where he has done this). But what he does say, like his more detailed thoughts on soap operas, challenges popular assumptions or the too easy dismissal of the significance of these forms of popular culture.

There is a complex relationship between rules, sport and the media. Football players in our society can be heroes or villains. Eric Cantona playing for Manchester United or Paul Gascoigne playing for England have been both, often within very short periods of time. Football is not only about rule-based social authority, it is also a spectacle, an image and a commodity. You can now buy 'football philosophers' T-shirts. Take your choice of slogans: one has the words of postmodernist Jean Baudrillard, 'Power is only too happy to make football bear a diabolical responsibility for stupefying the masses.' The replica goalkeeper top with novelist Albert Camus's name on it has the quote, 'All that I know most starkly about morality and obligations I owe to football.'[1]

As to soap opera, a recent TV reviewer identified two kinds of soap: one relies on 'strong women, big issues and social realism', like the UK's *EastEnders* and *Brookside*, and one relies on 'babes 'n' hunks, multiple couplings and hyperreality', *Melrose Place* from the USA being an example (*Observer*, 28 April 1996). The question then becomes how far these different forms can coexist. There is room, and we are talking about a postmodern era characterized by variety. But there is some indication of a shift away from the former to the latter.

As the soaps proliferate so to do confessional, Oprah Winfrey-style talk shows on TV. Is this the sort of thing Barry has identified as a manifestation of therapeutic culture, a growth of interest in emotional life and of the tendencies to self-reflection? Or is it an avenue for the expression of narcissism and an outward sign of individual and social emptiness. Barry is identifying a build-up of psychological stories, for example around politicians. As the therapeutic culture spreads the public are looking for stories about motivation and feelings in public figures and TV is increasingly willing and able to provide these. Now, he argues, the political is personal. A capacity to tolerate doubt and admit error has as much currency as a capacity to make tough decisions and stick to them. Andrew Samuels's chapter in this book argues that we might bring ambivalence out of disgrace and, in her chapter, Dorothy Rowe talks about a scientific culture in which relativity and uncertainty are accepted.

Ronald Reagan may have been the first US president to make a virtue out of indecisiveness. But his lack of concern with detail and his woolly-mindedness was achieved without irony. Bill Clinton is the first 'soft president'. Feature writer Jonathan Freedland describes him thus: 'He hugs men, he talks about his abusive stepfather, he shows his indecision and vulnerability in public ... In an era distrustful of the big idea, we can at least understand a man whose vocabulary is emotional, who begins every sentence with "I feel" not "I think"' ('Welcome to the 90s' *Elle*, September 1990, pp. 53–60).

Barry quotes Geoff Mulgan from the UK's independent 'think tank' Demos who believes we are in an 'anti-political age' in which the traditional domain of politics is increasingly unable to provide expression for a growing agenda including the rise of identity politics. It may be that some leaders are beginning to reflect the different politics that the end of certainty and the new age of anxiety provoke. But others stick rigidly to a stance that seeks to assert the unique truth claims of the particular position they hold. They emphasize that, although their intention may look to the ordinary person very similar to that of the opposing party, it is markedly different and undoubtedly right.

But if there is some change in the presentation of politics consistent with its softening or with the growth of an anti-political age, there is also the increasing development in politics, as in culture, of what George Steiner calls the 'universe of captions'. Political messages are packaged in the soundbites of slogans. The importance of public meetings, mass rallies and detailed debate has declined and been replaced by image consultants and market research.

Barry's chapter, though, serves to make us cautious of nostalgia or élitism in the way we look at contemporary cultural change. Public meetings and mass rallies have been manipulated and the energy of crowds harnessed to sinister aims, as has high culture, for example in Nazi Germany. Richard Hoggart's criticisms of soundbites is encapsulated by a Shakespeare quote he uses, 'The appetite grows by what it feeds on.' If that holds good for soundbite politicians, for Mozart's Greatest Hits or the shortened Jane Austen it also applies to, say, Wagner. The operatic works of Richard Wagner were criticized by Frankfurt School critical theorist Adorno (1981) because he saw the lure of theatrical unity they offered as disingenuous and ultimately totalitarian. Having posed questions about existence Wagner's art offers only itself as an answer. Wagner offers 'a synthesis of idealism and lust' and a 'trivializing of the world by profundity'.

The argument being developed here is that you might settle on accepting that both popular and high culture pose problems, the 'plague on both your houses' scenario. Or you can accept that, free of the cultural prescriptions of the past, we can choose. It is not that you have to enter into the sterile argument about how superior Shakespeare is to Bob Dylan. That is not a useful question. Indeed you should be able to confess to being both, say, a Wagnerian and someone in whom a range of emotions is engaged by American TV soaps *ER* and *NYPD Blue* (about, respectively, a hospital emergency room and a police precinct).

Barry's chapter connects with the concerns expressed by our other contributors and resonates with many of those things we encounter in our everyday life. His argument about the potential in popular culture to contribute to moral and rule-based communities directly addresses the question of 'living together' that is at the heart of this book. During the 'Euro 96' soccer tournament in England, in which popular culture, TV and football were juxtaposed as never before, one advertising poster said, 'Life's a Game, and we all know which one.' Nick Hornby's book about supporting Arsenal football club, *Fever Pitch* (1992), identifies the lure of football. It is the sense (sometimes) of being in the right place at the right time, of being at the heart of things. It is not about pleasure. Football clubs are 'extraordinarily inventive in the ways they find to cause their supporters sorrow'. But it is about belonging. Perhaps those people in the future, with whom these comments began, in their amazement at the crowd, hit the nail on the head.

Notes

1. With the possible exceptions of boxing and baseball, no sport has generated as many quotes as football. For the record, some people don't like the sport, George Orwell for one: 'Football has nothing to do with fair play. It is bound up with hatred,

jealousy, boastfulness, disregard of all rules and sadistic pleasure in witnessing violence; in other words, it is war minus the shooting' (written in 1945 and quoted in *The Picador Book of Sports Writing*, Picador, 1995)

References

Adorno, T. (1981), *In Search of Wagner*, Verso
Hornby, N. (1992), *Fever Pitch*, Gollancz

Chapter 6
IMPLICATIONS OF THE CHANGING WORLD OF WORK
Eric Miller

This chapter draws on the writer's experience and observations in a number of roles: as a consultant to organizations, large and small, in the public, private and voluntary sectors; as director of an educational programme that explores unconscious processes in groups and larger systems; as a member of OPUS (an Organization for Promoting Understanding in Society), which has since 1980 been trying to study underlying dynamics in British society; and finally as an individual citizen struggling to make sense of this rapidly changing world. The particular focus of the chapter is on the profound shift during the past fifteen years in the relatedness of the individual to the work organization – a process of psychological withdrawal. It attempts to analyse the key changes and to consider implications both for organization and management in the workplace and also for other areas of the individual's life. Finally it offers brief reflections on wider societal trends. We need first, however, to examine in some depth the nature of a person's psychological investment in work and other identities. And that takes us back to the earliest stages of development: the process through which a baby becomes a person.

Identity, individuality and self[1]

We confer an identity on the new baby as the daughter or son of proud parents, but it does not arrive with a sense of self. Mind and body, inside and outside, are merged together. It is perhaps best thought of as a bundle of primitive survival instincts and drives: seeking pleasure, nourishment, comfort, security – and avoiding pain. On this basis experiences are classified as either positive or negative, good or bad, and the shifts between them can be quite abrupt – from gurgles of pleasure to screams of pain and back again. When the milk is flowing the mother's breast represents bliss; when the baby is hungry or hurting the breast is felt to be malign, and we may see the baby attacking the breast with its tiny fists or arching away from it in fear. Because the associations are so diametrically opposed, these two aspects of the same breast are imprinted as quite different objects in the baby's mind – the 'good' breast and the 'bad' breast.

Consciousness of self seems to take several months to develop. It comes with gradual recognition of a boundary. Initially this is the physical boundary between infant and mother – the realization, for example, that this toe is mine and those arms are hers. What had previously been sensed perhaps as a vague continuum between nearer and further, with no distinction between feelings of pleasure or pain and their supposed causes, becomes a recognized difference between inside and outside. Otherness and selfhood define each other.

This is a disturbing discovery. It presents a new reality that does not fit the polarized picture formed during the early fight for survival. The baby is forced to recognize that the 'good breast' and the 'bad breast', which had been split apart in its mind, actually relate to one person – the mother. There is a dual experience of loss: loss of the idealized perfect mother; loss of that other image of the neglectful or sadistic mother. Because the baby has not quite yet learned to distinguish between wishes and actions, it is beset by anxiety that its impulses to attack the hated breast may actually destroy the mother, or may already have done so. Hence this step in development has been called the 'depressive position': the infant is pining for the lost loved object. At this stage there emerge the beginnings of guilt and reparation. Whereas earlier the young infant had been in a sense promiscuous – happy to be passed from one benign-looking person to another – now it will tend to cling to mother and to panic if she disappears for a moment, fearful that its destructive impulse will have driven her away for ever. Residues of that early separation anxiety get reactivated to a greater or lesser degree in most adults when, for example, they travel away from home or see a partner off on a journey – or leave a job.

The move to the depressive position is a significant step in emotional development, which reverberates through the rest of our lives. A few – the future psychopaths – never reach this position at all: they have no experience of guilt and the drive for reparation, which for most of us lead to a capacity for love and for secure relationships with others. To retain this more mature position requires reconsidering those powerfully contradictory perceptions of the mother, living with the ambivalent feelings and accepting that she is neither totally perfect nor totally malign but a mixture of less extreme qualities and frailties. Because of this complexity there is a continual urge to regress to the simpler world in which good was good and bad was bad. Each individual therefore develops a repertoire of defences to cope with the inconsistencies and contradictions. Splitting and denial in one guise or another are universal. The awkward unwanted part is projected on to others or repressed.

Progressively the child acquires and has to learn to manage a growing number of roles and identities. Starting within the family there is mother's child and father's child, which may mobilize two identities – two presentations of self – that are not entirely compatible with each other. Sibling, nephew/niece and grandchild are others. School evokes new identities, which bring out some parts of the self and suppress others. (It is not uncommon for middle-class children at a state school to speak with one accent and vocabulary in the playground and another at home.) School also provides new authority figures to relate to: teachers become screens on to which fragmented images of early experiences of parents can be projected, which often makes them larger than life.

Identity is a slippery word. Dictionaries offer two seemingly contradictory definitions: 'sameness' and 'individuality'. An identity card, for example, marks me out as unique, it tells me I am not the same as anyone else. But of course I have many identities, such as British, white male, husband and father, each of which I share with many others. Some I am born with; some I acquire or make for myself. So it is useful to think of one's individuality as a unique combination of samenesses on a very large number of dimensions.

Notions of sameness and difference are central to our social lives. And they are interdependent. There can be no sameness without a perceived difference, no self without other, no 'me' without a 'not-me'. So every identity implies both inclusion and exclusion. Logically such differences can be value-free. In practice some are: on a train, for example, the relationship between passengers and ticket inspector is usually neutral and impersonal. However, if there is a delay I may readily mobilize the identity of a maltreated passenger and treat him as a representative of an incompetent railway. Our primitive proclivity to turn difference into polarization is never far below the surface. If I need to feel good about myself on any dimension, the not-me has to be the receptacle of the bad. Superior and inferior, them and us, are the stuff of human relationships.

Hence the task of the self (the ego) in managing multiple identities is not simply a negotiation of interpersonal and inter-group relations: it is also a process at an unconscious level of negotiating the contradictions and conflicts within one's own inner world and dealing with the underlying anxiety that goes with them. By putting polarization into our external world we can reinforce our internal defences and protect ourselves from the pain of facing our inner ambivalence. We are engaged in a constant process of trying to export our inner chaos and to import order and predictability. And, outside, the institutions that we have been brought to rely on most for this predictability are family, school and workplace.

The individual and the work organization: 1975–95[2]

Although the term 'dependency culture' has been criticized, it is not an inaccurate description of Britain in the thirty years following the Second World War. The comprehensive welfare state, economic stability, rising prosperity, near-full employment, job security – all these had come to be taken for granted. Large employing institutions – the National Health Service, nationalized industries, big companies – accounted for a higher proportion of employment than in any other European country, and public sector norms of job security were imposed on the private sector employer through a combination of legislation and powerful unions: 'If mother showed signs of being less than generous with the breast, father could be relied upon to step in to keep the milk flowing' (Miller, 1986).

That image is not fanciful. The employing organization, with its hierarchical structure, provided security and met dependency needs. The job itself, even if not intrinsically satisfying, gave the individual a role and identity within a production system and a social grouping. Resentment at the enforced dependency – the other side of the ambivalence towards mother – and the need to express aggression and experience potency could be channelled through the union role. Thus the structures and relationships provided an orderly array of 'us's and 'not-me's among which the individual could deposit many of the diverse and often contradictory feelings in the inner world. In this way they reinforced the individual's defences.

Individuals therefore had a high degree of psychological investment in their work organizations – higher than they consciously realized – but by and large the organizations reciprocally furnished safe containers for the underlying anxieties.

That situation continued into the mid-1970s, when unemployment began to rise – from 2.6 to 5.4 per cent between 1974 and 1976 – and it stayed at that level until 1979, when the Thatcher government came in. Over the next three years it tripled. Manufacturing shed one-fifth of its remaining labour – nearly 1.5 million people. The number of long-term unemployed rose to over 1 million, a quarter of these being under twenty-five. Simultaneously various measures – cuts in education expenditure; a big increase in prescription charges; the ending of free school meals for children from low-income families, and many more – were beginning to trim the welfare state.

One justification for describing the previous period as a dependency culture was the shock when it ended. British society displayed the symptoms of 'failed dependency', the response of the baby suddenly abandoned by mother. One continuing theme was withdrawal and retreat from reality and flight into a world of fantasy: more than ever, films and plays offered escape to a supernatural future or to a mythical, magical past – an imagined golden age of early infancy – presenting the archetypal struggle between good and evil. Then there was heightened fear of the nuclear holocaust, an unimaginable horror against which the individual was totally impotent – a fear no doubt justified, but again resonating with an infantile fantasy. Impotence generated rage, which was enacted, for example, by major riots in Liverpool and London in 1981. Finally, the Falklands crisis produced a real enemy for everyone to hate and attack – and the incidence of suicides and industrial disputes dropped sharply. Running through all this was people's loss of trust in the established institutions that they felt had betrayed them: the state, the employing institutions and the unions that had failed to protect the workers from the 'wicked' employers. At the same time the other main institutions that cater for dependency – the church and the family – were themselves losing ground.

For very many individuals redundancy was a shattering experience. Hardest hit were the 'company towns' or villages where the main source of work – factory or mine – was shut; but there were casualties elsewhere. Just as important as loss of income, if not more so, was loss of structure, of status, and of self-esteem. A not uncommon result was loss of sexual potency. Interviewed in a study in West Yorkshire in 1983, some women said that 'a man's not a real man without a job', and they meant it literally (Khaleelee and Miller, 1984). Many men (and virtually all the casualties were men) were described as drifting aimlessly. It seemed that for them the work identity had been fused with self. With that taken away, they had no self to govern their internal world and to mobilize other latent identities – not even husband and father. In the main their withdrawal had been involuntary, though some who had been tempted by voluntary redundancy packages also became lost souls.

Withdrawal of investment in the workplace was widespread among those who remained there. 'Keep your head down', 'Don't stick your neck out', 'Keep your nose clean', 'Cover your arse': these were the prescriptions for survival in what was now a dangerous setting – 'Whose turn next?' – and the physical language implied that one's actual body was felt to be at risk. Instead of identifying with the organization, employees were falling back on to smaller groupings to support the individual's identity and need to find meaning. There was a tendency to obliterate those who had left and even to gain some identity and sense of superiority from being the non-unemployed.

For the unemployed not all was gloom. Some went into business themselves: they reported that they tended to work harder but to get more satisfaction from it. Others again made a livelihood through a mix of activities, often in the black economy and drawing state benefits to provide a basic income. Some of these, however, were less driven by money than by pursuing their own interests: for example, making music, further education, doing voluntary work, campaigning. Finally there was the mixed model of taking up different roles and different activities at different phases of one's life: full-time employment, chosen interests, part-time jobs and so on. This of course has been a typical model for women, with child-rearing as the chosen activity. There is no doubt that the availability of motherhood as a significant, indeed central, identity generally made redundancy much less devastating for them than for men.

By the mid-1980s the trauma was diminishing. Unemployment had fallen a little. The long-running national soap opera of the 1984–5 miners' strike provided wonderful support for our schizoid defences: either Scargill or Thatcher could be chosen as the hero to identify with or the villain to be denigrated, and the country divided around them. (The Brighton bombing then muddled these projections by making the IRA the aggressor and Thatcher the victim, and support for the miners dwindled.) The economy was beginning to recover and as it turned into a mini-boom memories of the beginning of the decade began to fade. For the million or more long-term unemployed, of whom many of the younger ones had never been in work, this was little consolation, but they were becoming a taken-for-granted phenomenon. Businesses were expanding again, jobs started to feel more secure, and perhaps the 1979 recession had been a temporary and necessary blip on the way to the Thatcher promised land of prosperity.

1989 abruptly put paid to that fantasy. Although some middle managers had lost their jobs in the early 1980s, when 'flattening the hierarchy' was coming into favour, it was the blue-collar workers who were mainly affected; and indeed the reinvigoration of their working-class identities helped many to sustain a sense of self-worth. In that respect the opportunity to identify with the striking miners in 1984–5 was an added fillip. From 1989 onwards the white-collars – the voters for Thatcher – bore their full share. For some of these individuals it was possibly even more devastating than it had been for their working-class counterparts ten years earlier.

One type of business that expanded as a result was outplacement – helping redundant managers to find new jobs. In 1992 I lunched with the managing director of one such firm and he told me that he was off that afternoon to 'do a pick-up'. I looked puzzled. He explained that at 4.00 p.m., though they didn't yet know it, three very senior executives of [a well-known company] were to be told they were redundant and he would be on hand. Sometimes the shock was such that people literally had to be picked up. Outplacement counselling could involve weeks or months of psychological rehabilitation before clients were fit to re-enter the job market.

That feeling of betrayal is still quite a common response to redundancy, but it is probably diminishing and also less intense. The organization is now a demonstrably less reliable 'mother'. British Telecom and other privatized utilities made thousands or even tens of thousands at a time redundant. Few if any spheres of employment – whether in the civil service, university teaching or the health services, let alone the private sector – can realistically be perceived as secure. In September 1995 it was reported that more than 2 million people – nearly one in ten of all employees – had been made redundant in the previous two years and had had to seek alternative employment.

The response has been a much deeper and more permanent psychological withdrawal from the work organization. Cynicism is widespread. The individual's relatedness to the organization is now much more instrumental. Compliance is seen as the safest strategy for survival: do as you're told and never question authority. A term heard recently is 'calculated sincerity'. Needs for attachment and dependency are lodged in small groups or individuals, not in the organization.

An increasing number of employees make contingency plans for redundancy, so that when they collect their pay-off a head-hunter may well have the next job lined up for them. That especially applies to those at or near the top of the organization – those who take on the surgical task of down-sizing, delayering, or 'right-sizing', to use the latest euphemisms. They have already negotiated their three-year rolling contracts, share options and platinum handshakes. Those near the bottom also see redundancy as a real possibility but they have no such buffer and the prospect of an unpayable mortgage on a depreciated house does much to encourage their compliance.

Implications for organization and management

Originally the stated and often genuine intention behind flattening the hierarchy was to increase empowerment: fewer levels would lead to more direct communication between bottom and top. Many of today's pyramids do indeed have fewer levels but are actually experienced as steeper, more like pagodas, with an invisible and inaccessible top management ensconced in a celestial tip. The perceived height of the pagoda is correlated with the differentials of remuneration. A dozen years ago the pay of the chief executive of a medium-to-large British company was ten or twelve times the shop-floor average; now it can be fifty or a hundred times. This is so inconsistent with the rhetoric of empowerment that we need to understand how it has come about.

One plausible explanation is that in times of danger followers are prepared to surrender themselves to a leader as, in Freud's term, an 'ego-ideal' who offers salvation in the fight against an external enemy. The more remote the figurehead, the easier it is to weave myths about him. That is how Hitler was created. What we actually observe in practice, however, is a disconnection between top and bottom in these large enterprises. It seems that the significant leader–follower relationship lies elsewhere. Critical here is the power of external stakeholders – for businesses these are the banks and the big institutional investors. It is they who have the power to appoint the leader; it is they who are looking for the saviour with the vision to safeguard their loans and investments; and it is they who are the followers whose hope for salvation the leader has to maintain. As for the common enemy, the focus is on cutting costs; wages and salaries are a major expense, and so in this formulation the employees become the surrogate enemy. The paradox is that mobilization of internal followers would seem to be a necessary condition for the survival and prosperity of the enterprise, while at the same time their unconscious rage against the leadership has become conscious – not repressed but quite consciously suppressed and not easily diverted on to other targets. They are well aware that the savings on the first hundred redundancies merely pay the salary of the new chief executive. Early in 1995, Sir Iain Vallance, chairman of BT, asserted in a letter to the *Financial Times* that the 'precise level of the remuneration of the chief executive is surely immaterial' to employees. Commentators were quick to tell him how much he was out of touch.

While the managements of almost all organizations recognize the importance of mobilizing commitment of the work force and many espouse empowerment, their actual responses suggest that the significant shift in the relatedness of the individual to the organization is unrecognized. Vallance's statement, for example, implies unawareness that attitudes of BT's employees might have changed as a result of losing a third of their former colleagues. And this is a big difference between the early 1980s and the early 1990s: the survivors can no longer deny their vulnerability by 'forgetting' those who have gone. Other managements recognize that they have to do something to achieve and maintain commitment, and so there has been a plethora of training programmes, mission statements, empowerment schemes and so forth. In these attempts they often seem to be equating commitment to the task of the enterprise with loyalty to its management. Employees almost invariably see it as the latter and become more cynical. Loyalty to a management that has been profoundly disloyal to thousands of erstwhile employees is a laughable notion. The training is dismissed, often with justification, as an attempt at indoctrination, the mission as empty verbiage, and empowerment as meaningless in a setting where to question the view of one's superior is to risk losing one's job.

Most managements seem nevertheless to have reacted in one of those two ways: either denial that there is an issue to be addressed, or adopting a strategy of retrieving loyalty through persuasion. These responses express two familiar mental models long held by managers:

- that employees are interchangeable mechanisms that have no feelings; or
- that employees are like children who will believe what their parents tell them.

It may well be that managements have underestimated the degree of psychological withdrawal that lies behind the front of compliance because they had become accustomed to seeing the union as a barometer of disaffection; but of course the unions, particularly in industry and commerce, are now much less responsive instruments.

Why do those familiar models no longer work? One reason lies in the definition of 'the organization' itself. 'The organization' has never been an objective entity that can be seen and touched. It is essentially a construct in the minds of people who perceive themselves as inside it or outside. But at least there has been a shared definition of the boundary. Today the familiar phrase, 'belonging to an organization', with its reciprocal connotations of proprietary ownership on the one side and emotional involvement and commitment on the other, is obsolescent and the boundaries more problematic. Outsourcing is one factor: tasks previously done by employees are contracted out. (A further complication is that in some cases – for example, cleaning – the same job is done by the same people but they are now employed by a private contractor.) Use of agency workers is widespread: the Health Service, for example, is heavily reliant on agency nurses. Some of them are employed in one hospital by day and hired by an agency to do night shifts in another hospital. To which of these three organizations do they 'belong'? The number of part-time workers has greatly increased, the majority of them women. In industry there is a growing tendency to involve engineers from supplying companies in the product–design teams of their customers. The once clear boundaries between inside and outside have become blurred. Add to these factors the iterative processes of restructuring many systems and the accompanying transfer and turnover of personnel and one can see why any shared construct of 'the organization' is becoming so tenuous. Consequently, what had once served as a relatively stable structured system of defences against anxiety has, with a few exceptions, disappeared. In many cases it seems to have disaggregated into small, safe, half-hidden clusters, not necessarily united by a shared task but mostly coming together around a shared insecurity and a resentment of their enforced compliance plus shared feelings of hatred and/or contempt towards top management. If 'the organization' survives at all with a mothering function, as a container it is at best a very leaky colander.

If this is a reasonably accurate picture of contemporary enterprises it is clear that managements need another mental model to mobilize commitment and empowerment. And for many, success depends on it. Psychological withdrawal implies that people merely enact roles: they do not live them. Moreover, in a culture of compliance the workforce acts on the belief that survival is dependent on maintaining the *status quo*. Any criticisms, reservations and above all creative ideas that they might have are felt to threaten the *status quo* and therefore tend to be censored. Yet these are just the resources that the enterprise needs if it is to engage effectively with the unpredictable environment of today and tomorrow. At the same time, because of the combination of reduced headcounts – doing your redundant colleague's job as well as your own – and the advances in technology, especially IT, a larger proportion of roles in most enterprises are highly demanding or pivotal for effectiveness, and often both. These require psychological presence.[3] In other words, the need is for people to invest themselves fully in these roles, to be totally preoccupied with them, to own them.

We can state two of the key conditions that make this possible. One is that the role is defined in such a way that the task itself and the working relationships around it can be experienced as meaningful and genuinely recognized as valuable. The other is that the system has to be experienced as safe in the sense that the individual can take authority and know that his/her voice will be heard and respected even if the content of the message might be disturbing for the status quo. In other words it is a system of distributed leadership, in which authority is derived from the task rather than from hierarchical status.

Some enterprises are making moves in this direction. For example, there is increasing adoption of business process re-engineering which has the effect of reallocating roles into more horizontal structures. But there is one difficulty that most managements find it hard to accept. They can provide the conditions to make psychological presence possible but they cannot make it happen. Only the individual can choose how much of the self to invest in that identity. And there is a further uncertainty. Given the rate of change which almost all enterprises are facing, even the most well-intentioned and sophisticated managements will be unable to provide stable systems that serve as defences against anxiety. Indeed their inherent instability is more likely to generate anxiety. We shall have a little more to say about these issues in the sections that follow.

Implications for the individual

In the traditional work organization, which is still far from obsolete, the position of the individual employees is remarkably similar to that of the peasants and serfs of medieval England. Their superiors lay on them the obligation to perform obediently the duties of the station in life to which God/top management has called them. The individual's status is defined by the worker role which locks her/him into a particular set of interpersonal and intergroup relations that acquires its own culture, its own defences. As we have indicated, a major factor that sustained this archaic structure for so long was that it represented a macro-version of the family: the organization as mother met the dependency needs of the employee. Mother's love, however, was conditional: do your duty or you don't get fed. Enforced dependency generates rage. Workers now are a good deal more prosperous than in the days of Marx, but alienation – the experience of being forced to do something that gives one little satisfaction by someone else who has coercive powers and steals most the fruits of one's labours – has by no means disappeared.

> The coercive hold that the organization has over the individual, whether 'manager' or 'worker', is that it satisfies his dependent needs and his infantile greed, though it does so indirectly by offering the pseudo-autonomy of the consumer role. As a consumer, to be sure, he has choices; but the orchestrated pressure to spend and consume is still a secondary coercion that reinforces dependency on an employing organization, which is to be placated through passivity and compliance ... The individual's rage and his wishes – not always unconscious – to destroy the organization have to be suppressed or repressed (Miller, 1986, pp. 263–4).

One defence, as we have seen, was the fusion of the work identity with self and those who adopted it were the most traumatized by redundancy.

Alienation began to become more overt in the 1980s; compliance was more conscious and cynicism about 'management' could be acknowledged, at least in private. Such an instrumental relationship is plainly less unhealthy than a blind absorption in a dependency culture. It also opens up the possibility of choice. As we noted earlier, today's enterprises need people to be psychologically present, but this is something they have to be in a position to choose. The less dependent they are for their livelihood on that particular employer – in other words, if they are confident that they can sell their skills elsewhere – then the freer they are to invest themselves fully into their roles. Their needs for security are met from within themselves, from their own competence. They have achieved what in the 1960s and 1970s was the goal of self-actualization – the opposite pole of dependency within the traditional feudal structures. They are self-employed in a quite literal sense even though they are on the payroll. And like many successful people who are self-employed in the more conventional sense they derive great satisfaction from the work itself. The proportion of the working population who are 'self-employed' in these two senses is increasing and will continue to do so as employers learn to value the contribution that they can make.

How are their dependency needs met? For some it is from a secure home – parents, spouse, family. They can be autonomous adults in their work identity if there is a safe space elsewhere for the more fragile parts of themselves. Others can appropriately be described as 'self-contained', in that they do not need mother or family or organization to provide containment; they provide it from within.

The mature self-contained adult has had the kind of parenting that has made it possible to internalize a 'good mother', to work through the ambivalence of the depressive position and to manage the anxieties generated by internal contradictions and conflicts. For those whose early experience has been less favourable, psychotherapy can contribute to this process. Not that the process is ever complete; but the mature individual exports less internal chaos into the external world and has less need of external supports for the internal defences. Such a person can be described as having a strong moral skeleton – a robust self that is confident about the difference between right and wrong, is not easily swayed by group pressures and conveys an inner solidity.

There is a second and less healthy version of self-containment, and one becoming increasingly prevalent, which is individualism. For Shakespeare, 'to thine own self be true' was an injunction to do what you know to be right. In the twentieth century the most likely interpretations would be either 'let it all hang out' or 'do what's in your own best interests' – two versions of individualism. They seem to be the products of two quite different developmental processes. The former is associated with lack of defences. In contrast with the mature person, in which the self as it were manages the multiple identities of the individual, bringing forward those parts of the inner world that are appropriate to a particular identity and holding others in check, here the self is porous or barely present at all: there is little or no filtering between a stimulus and the response. People with these characteristics may make a significant contribution in, for example, research organizations where creative lateral thinking is valued and their associated eccentricities are accepted, but are unlikely to survive elsewhere. Self-interested individualism, on the other hand, is a product of an array of defences based on narcissism which make it possible to maintain the infant's sense of omnipotence, of being at the centre of the world, of being the world. Such an individualist can be psychologically present in the sense of being fully there, but all the energy is directed to self-interest – a self unencumbered by such complications as guilt and reparation. Thus there may be a front of high commitment but this is not to the role, the organization or relationships. Individualists of this kind can appear impressive and their egocentricity readily gets them promoted to leadership positions, in which they can do a great deal of damage; and they are usually clever and self-interested enough to move on with a generous severance package before the damage becomes evident.

Wider implications

Self-interested individualism is not new: it has long been seen as linked to the growth of the consumer society, though it has certainly been accelerated since 1980 by the Thatcherite philosophy. Similarly, the erosion of established institutions such as the church and the family has been going on over a much longer period. Incidence of crime rose rapidly during the 1980s and early 1990s, though it is possibly starting to stabilize at a much higher level. Cynicism about the political process and the relevance of government in addressing the country's socio-economic problems followed a similar curve but has escalated during the 1990s as the corrupt use of power for personal gain has become more widespread or at any rate more manifest; and when a government can impose a policy such as rail privatization that is opposed by 80 per cent of the electorate the term 'democracy' has a hollow ring. Distrust of employing organizations has displayed a similar trajectory and it evidently both feeds and is fed by these other trends.

Socially it may also be the most significant. As we have seen, millions of individuals have been deprived – some of them permanently – of an identity that had been a major component in their sense of self, and a host of young people have not acquired a work identity at all. The loss of stable structures to meet needs for dependency and for defences against anxiety means that the corresponding parts of the individual – essentially unconscious parts – have been made homeless as it were. New receptacles are required for projections of the unwanted elements and new safe houses for the attachment needs. Dependency and impotence can generate a readiness to follow any leadership, whether moral or immoral, that seems to promise salvation or at least survival. One recent example was willing corruption of young women by a priest in Yorkshire. Another was the woman who sacrificed her life to prevent the export of calves to the European mainland.

Naturally, too, there is a wish for a leader at the macro-level to find the solution. Whose wish is not altogether clear. The following of Tony Blair, who at the time of writing (October 1995) is being set up as a saviour, seems to comprise those who feel threatened by the marginalized sections of the population rather than the marginalized themselves.

However, one must be cautious about generalizations. Certainly for very many people the loss of stable structures is leading, on the one hand, to a search for alternative and sometimes bizarre leaderships and, on the other hand, to an over-determined individualism. Add to that one's day-to-day experiences – accosted by homeless beggars on the streets, bombarded by media stories of crime and violence, hearing of friends losing their jobs and houses – it is all too tempting to feel that we are the victims of a unique upheaval and that all the things we valued are going to be destroyed. Indeed, in writing this chapter I found myself at times caught up in a primitive splitting process of identifying with 'the betrayed' against 'the betrayers'. This is not the first upheaval that we as a society have gone through in this century. Some of us have memories of two world wars and the great depression in between. And all the time the 'we' changes. While the older generation is mourning what was – the 'we' who 'never had it so good' – a younger generation is grappling with what is. Not brought up to expect secure employment for life, they are adapted to change, find their own ways of meeting their attachment needs and their own sets of 'them's and 'us's, and are often more internally secure and self-confident than many of 'us' were. Clearly some of us, or parts of most of us, want a national leader to be our saviour. And certainly there are some measures that need the impetus of a national government initiative. Employment and education are obvious examples. If a Labour government is elected and if a referendum supported proportional representation then that might undermine the adversarial political system which, besides having become a joke, produces policies based on dogma rather than constructive argument about tackling key issues. Meanwhile, however, the reparative sense of obligation to one's fellow beings – the sense of community – is alive and well and generating a host of small, often local, positive initiatives that are too little recognized. For example:

1. *The Big Issue*, now distributed in provincial cities as well as London, enables homeless people to regain self-respect

through earning money from selling the magazine and provides stepping-stones to homes and jobs.

2. A major national retail chain gives employees financial help to pursue educational and other personal developmental activities of their own choice. They may acquire qualifications that could enable them to take jobs elsewhere. If they stay, the existence of choice makes it more possible to be 'psychologically present'. If they leave, they demonstrate to others that one need not be stuck.

3. A north London school with a high proportion of Afro-Caribbean under-achievers has created a comprehensive mentoring scheme. The voluntary mentors are black men and women who have been successful in a wide range of fields. They work with both child and family, as well as the school, to encourage motivation to learn and at the same time they serve as role models to channel students' aspirations.

These initiatives and hundreds more help the individual to acquire a more positive and mature sense of self and to use it in constructive ways. They will probably have more effect in shaping the future of our society than the action of government.

Notes

1. The perspective on infant development in this section owes much to the theories of Melanie Klein: see, for example, Klein (1952, 1959).
2. The first part of the analysis in this section draws particularly on the work of OPUS (OPUS 1980–89; Khaleelee and Miller, 1985; Miller 1986,1993).
3. See Kahn (1992).

References

Kahn, W. A. (1992), 'To be Fully There: Psychological Presence at Work', *Human Relations*, 45, pp. 321–50

Khaleelee, O. and Miller, E. J. (1984), *The Future of Work: A Report of the West Yorkshire Talkabout, July–November 1983*, Work & Society,

– (1985), 'Beyond the Small Group: Society as an Intelligible Field of Study', in M. Pines (ed.), *Bion and Group Psychotherapy*, Routledge & Kegan Paul, pp. 353–83.

Klein, M. (1952), 'Some Theoretical, Conclusions, Regarding the Emotional Life of the Infant', in M. Klein, P. Heimann, S. Isaacs and J. Rivière (eds.), *Developments in Psychoanalysis*, Hogarth, pp. 198–236.

– (1959), 'Our Adult World and Its Roots in Infancy', *Human Relations*, 12, pp. 291–303, Also in M. Klein, *Our Adult World and Other Essays*, Heinemann, 1963, pp. 1–22.

Miller, E. J. (1986), 'Making Room for Individual Autonomy', in S. Srivastva and Associates, *Executive Power*, San Francisco, CA: Jossey-Bass, pp. 257–88

– (1993), 'Power, Authority, Dependency and Cultural Change', in *From Dependency to Autonomy: Studies in Organization and Change*, Free Association Books, pp. 284–315.

OPUS (1980–89), Bulletin, Nos. 1–26, OPUS

Commentary
TOO MUCH, THE WRONG SORT, OR NONE AT ALL – WORK IN THE 1990S

A Russian *émigré* now living in the thriving Russian colony of New York, in a radio interview, described the problem of being in a city where people just worked all the time. 'It is as if work is their Gulag,' he said. Work, or the absence of work, is so much at the core of all our lives. It seems we either have nothing or too much. At the very least we are aware that the world of work is one area where there is no doubt that changes are immense. This is the area addressed in Eric Miller's chapter.

But Eric is not just surveying the changing scene. He is saying things about the resonance of work and changes in our relation to work for our sense of self, our capacity to know who we are and to be secure in that. What happens when that sense of dependency on, and identification with, the place we work ends? Eric seeks to examine this using the insights of Melanie Klein, gained via her study of early infant development. The chapter is thus both an examination of a key area of social change and an illustration of the insights into such change from one school of psychoanalysis.

Sociologists talk about the advent of post-Fordism or even about the McDonaldization of society (Ritzer, 1995). These will be discussed in more detail in our conclusion. But the breakdown of big firms and the dispersal of production to all corners of the world is familiar to everyone – just look at your car: clutch from Korea, bumpers from Spain, windows from France, assembled in Essex. As to the McDonaldization idea, the colonization of more and more of the world not just by the burger but by firms using the same methods is the sort of phenomenon that could fruitfully be used if someone wanted to remake Charlie Chaplin's film about production-line factories, *Modern Times*, for the 1990s

The Thatcher years in the UK heralded a customer revolution. It encouraged the right to complain. In so doing it increased the stress of those providing services, the need to get it right, no room for mistakes. When you put this alongside the development in the same period of short-term contracts and performance-related pay it becomes clear how we imprison people in uncertainty and stress.

Many surveys have been carried out into aspects of the impact of changes in work on the pattern and well-being of people's lives. Present trends allow us to predict that almost one person in ten of those currently in work will lose their jobs over the next three years. Most people can expect to be made redundant at least once in the course of their careers. Growing numbers of people live with what we can call serial redundancy, having lost jobs four or five times. Much of the publicity about job loss in the 1990s concentrates on its impact on the middle class but it is salutary to note that unemployment rates amongst miners a year after losing their jobs was around 46 per cent. Those who did find work saw wages drop on average by 30 per cent. Only 3 per cent became self-employed.

A survey of 1,300 middle to senior managers found that 81 per cent 'often or always' work longer than their official hours; 54 per cent 'often or always' 'work in the evenings and 36 per cent 'often or always' work at weekends. Seven out of ten British workers report that they want to work a forty-hour week but only three out of ten do so. But it is not this, and its impact on their health and family life, that most worries them. What is uppermost in their minds is not having this job in the near future; 58 per cent of middle managers report not feeling in control of their future career development.

Down-sizing, short-term contracts, contract or freelance careers and portfolio working are now everyday terms. They can mean very different things to individuals. For example, portfolio working can be either having a number of jobs, sometimes simultaneously, sometimes consecutively, over a period of a number of years, by choice or by necessity. The jobs might be so badly paid or insecure that you have to keep as many going at the same time as possible. This is a far cry from the picture of the freedom of choice and the excitement of new challenges that can also be encapsulated in the term portfolio working. In 1871, John Ruskin said that, 'in order that people may be happy in their work, these things are needed: they must be fit for it; they must not do too much of it; and they must have a sense of success in it.'[1] While these observations may remain true the trajectory of change in the world of work makes these elusive goals. Amidst all the rhetoric and the shifting terminology we must not underestimate the extent and the impact, socially and personally, of losing your job.

When we think of the future we encounter people talking of a different idea of what work is likely to be. The UK's Labour Party leader Tony Blair now talks of 'employment security' as opposed to 'job security'. Jobs are being created but it might mean more part-time work for more people. In 1984 there were 4 million women in part-time work and 570,000 men, by 1994 the figures were respectively 5 million and 990,000. This may impact on gender balances in terms of who works out of the home and who is involved in home and family care. It might be that as technology develops the potential for the 'virtual organization', linking people electronically means we do not so readily equate work with a sense of physical place. It seems certain that the future of work will involve more change, more transitions for each worker than has previously been the norm, with the concomitant need for individuals to plan across the breaks and changes. The retraining society is not cosy. There will be a need for us all to deal with the anxiety that even if things had always worked out, just about, in the past they might not next time you find yourself made redundant, or for this writer, the next time your research contract runs out.[2]

While there might be grounds for disagreement as to future patterns of work, the changing patterns now, and the fears of the future, certainly do contribute to the anxious society so many of our contributors have talked about. It is far from that idea of an inner connection of the person with the organization they work for that was one model from the past. The 'decline of corporate man' has been linked to the prominence of finance capital in the UK. It is the movement of money rather than the production of goods which takes centre stage. Global money markets, the transfer electronically of huge sums of money and the speculation around shifting exchange rates are the stuff of everyday news. But they do seem to separate money from production, from factories and jobs. It is in this environment that there is an end of allegiance either of the firm to you, or you to it.

The 1995 takeover in the pharmaceutical industry of Wellcome by Glaxo prompted one Wellcome employee to write that this had led to the demise of perhaps one of the last examples of profitable, paternalistic capitalism with a moral base. Wellcome was closely linked with Dartford in Kent, maybe not like a pit village was linked with its pit, but still enough that the firm was tied into the fabric and history of the place. Most of the staff, according to this employee, thought that they were relatively badly paid but they traded that for job security, humanitarian management and a sense that the largest shareholder, the Wellcome Trust, was committed to the advancement of medicine (A. R. Bevan in the *Guardian*, 9 September 1995).

Eric points us to the laughable conceit by which managers request loyalty from workers while they exhibit none themselves. But the sorts of shift this represents must impact on the way individuals meet their needs for dependency, to find a place to both identify with and be contained by. He has presented for us in his chapter an account, necessarily very condensed, of Melanie Klein's account of infant development and the formation of identity. Many psychoanalytic writers emphasize the emotional need for both intimacy and separation, Bowlby and Winncott for example. Klein underlined that recognition of ambivalence in us all. It is manifest in the wish to be dependent and the destructive rage we can feel if we are vulnerable and helpless.

The impact of this shake-up in the way we relate to our place of work is, in Eric's argument, potentially positive. But the dilemma must be in balancing the two opposing effects of this impact: first, being set free from the conventional ties of work can be liberating, and, second, work provided some sense of security, met some dependency needs. If only those who are relatively secure can benefit from the new insecurities it is possible to develop this into a strong-get-stronger argument that is not inconsistent with the tenor of the times. The all pervasive performance principle has little room for ambivalence, compassion or forgiveness. An example of this, couched in terms of putting the user/customer first, was when Tony Blair spoke of the Labour Party's programme for improving standards in schools as having 'zero toleration of failure in teachers'.

The image of the split person has been with us a long time. Melanie Klein was identifying things that, albeit in different ways, have been examined in literature and philosophy for many years. In Pat Barker's trilogy of novels about the First World War she describes a 'fugue personality' in which front-line soldiers can split off life in the trenches from the rest of their lives. 'You can only do it if you don't think about it' is one explanation the soldiers offer.[3] With a world of work characterized by anxiety and by no sense of allegiance or identification one can see a whole society living this sort of fugue life.

Another way forward, taken up by a number of contributors to the book, Bob Hinshelwood and Andrew Samuels included, is the emphasis on the small scale. Coming together around a shared concern and activity offers the possibility for growth in an individual's felt autonomy and also offers a safe space to put some of our needs for attachment and dependence. As such this contrasts with a false route of following the self-interested individualism that is so much lauded.

Eric's examination of work can also be linked with those questions about other areas of the individual's life that are considered in Susie Orbach's and Valerie Sinason's chapters. What happens to parenting? How can these shifts in work be assimilated with, for example, the role fathers can play in child-care? Of course, the possibilities here are contradictory – an increase in the numbers of hours worked and more stress in those hours on the one hand, and on the other, shifts to part-time work and the reality of career breaks (perhaps not chosen) for all. There is at least now more discussion of the interconnections between work and the rest of life, as is evident in this book, in the press and even in conferences. In July 1996, for example, the Employment Policy Institute sponsored a conference called 'Love and Work' in which questions to be explored included: How important are jobs to sustaining secure friendships and relationships and to being able to love?

In Dorothy Rowe's chapter she speaks of the impact that a concern with nouns rather than verbs has. Postmodern organization theory suggests we see organization as a verb and not a noun (Parker, 1992). If we stop assuming that an organization is a physical place and see it as people coming together around a shared activity then we might have more scope for the creative. Then, if we think of the 'self' as a verb...who knows, it may be all in the words!

Notes

1. Ruskin is quoted in Cary Cooper, 'Hot under the Collar', *Times Higher Education Supplement*, 21 June 1996.
2. Of the many reports into changing work this section draws on a selection published in 1995/6: The Coalfield Communities Campaign; Institute of Management's 'Survival of the Fittest'; Institute for Employment Studies and Careers Research and Advisory Centre, 'Managing Careers in 2000 and beyond'.
3. Pat Barker's trilogy is made up of *Regeneration* (1991), *The Eye in the Door* (1993) and *The Ghost Road* (1995) and is published by Penguin Books.

References

Ritzer, Georg,e (1995), *The McDonaldization of Society*, Pine Forge Press
Parker, Martin, (1992), 'Post-Modern Organizations or Postmodern Organization Theory?' in *Organization Studies*

Chapter 7
I HAVE AN IDEA . . .
R. D. Hinshelwood

> I cannot perch upon that rim of sky
> to search my world of corn and sand
> on which my feet now stand
>
> > The Horizon's Lure, unknown poet

Introduction

Someone said, 'Beware of a politician with an idea.' But a politician needs more than an idea, he needs a group of supporters and voters to get the idea too. It needs to proliferate through a crowd. It is a bit like the flu. And yet having an idea is not *felt* to be a disease. On the contrary, it gives the exhilaration of conviction, a climactic sense of having a 'truth'. An idea has a natural progress from the mind of an individual, to become the core of a group. Otherwise it dies. With its promotion to a single-minded consuming passion, for its group of holders the entire world falls into place around the selected idea. Conflicts and other bits of misplaced litter in life become easily dealt with by the guiding principle of the idea. This pattern – the idea with its surrounding followers and its political consequences – is, loosely, what we call an 'ideology'. The creation of ideology appears to be a bedrock of life in a group.

We tend, instinctively, to suspect ideology, and for good reason.

I agreed to make a contribution to this collection of essays on the condition that it was not going to be a passion-piece about how psychoanalysis can come up with the idea that will make our society different, cure its ills, a new ideology looking for its gathering of supporters. I would like this piece to be a calm reflection; to be *about* politics though not *of* it. That cannot be. I cannot be outside of political debate.

The problem of 'position' is central to the theme of this essay. There is nowhere outside the global culture from where we can view the problem and its solutions, and no one in that nowhere. Yet there is always a queue of people claiming to be in that objective position. Indeed I argue that one of the prime causes of our difficulties is that so much of politics is done as if someone was looking in from outside.

In this essay I want to explore what a non-objective approach might look like; that is to say, a return to a politics looked at *from the inside*. But a return that has been marked by a new understanding of human beings. This exploration will entail quite a speedy traverse across a number of problems that people set themselves by aggregating together in societies. These include the problematic entanglement of passions with ideas that creates ideology; the mistaken solutions of pluralism on the one hand and of neutral fence-sitting on the other; and the quest for a different balance between these two – emotions and reason – in our political life.

Culturally we separate out, like oil and water, our emotions from reason. Emotions are recognizably of a moment and of a place; while reason claims a lofty independence and universality. Emotions are of a person, reason has a generality. Because of such polarities, they become each other's worst enemy. Animals have passions, and computers reason. We need a blend. Or rather we need a new blend, not the old impassioned ideas claiming reasonableness while driven by unacknowledged emotions. The quest for a different balance between emotions and reason must, I claim, be our new politics.

The problem

Our start must be this most dangerous period in human history, our generation's half-century poised for mutual nuclear destruction. It has been based in the ideas of Russian communism versus the crusading capitalist idealism of the West. Indeed the twentieth century has been especially prone to economic ideas and ideologies. From the Stalinist degradation of communism to the fascism of Hitler and Japan, to the multitude of nationalist conflagrations which recently have seen spitefully inhuman attitudes destroy people in the Falklands, in Kuwait and the Gulf, and in Bosnia, as well as in so many impoverished third World countries, we have been captured by ideas more than at any time since medieval theology tyrannized the post-Roman Europe. Ideas are the enemies of humans, so it would seem, despite the hunger we have for their poison.

Collecting together

Why is the Western world degenerating into a high-tech version of the squabbling city-states of ancient Greece? Have no lessons been learned? Probably it is not so simple. It is more than just the cussedness of individual human beings with a good idea in their heads which they can't let go of. It is in our rapidly expanding collectives that new problems of co-operation are encountered. The advance of technology, especially transport and communications, has brought together ever larger collectives of individual human beings. The ever wider net of communications, and the ever faster response times, ensure that ever larger numbers of people are drawn under the spell of good ideas. And this occurs at the very same time as larger numbers of people need to be drawn into co-operation with each other, rather than conflict.

Whether or not there is something inherently destructive in the individual human being from the beginning, there is something which is inherently destructive in human society. We must go to the human collective to understand these phenomena. Nietzsche asserted: 'Insanity in individuals is something rare: in nations, parties and epochs it is the rule.' And we are familiar with the fact that individuals may be good losers, but groups almost never are. The splitting of collectives of human beings into sects, factions, parties, classes, nations and blocs, is different from the psychology of the individual human.

What therefore happens in a collection of humans, when it becomes possessed of an idea? A kind of identity takes them over. People can be consumed by the idea of their group, and in the end become its vehicles for expression. Cults can proceed to the actual bodily destruction of the people that make it up – from the mass suicide at Masada in the first century, to the suicide pilots of Japan in 1945, to the Branch Davidian sect at Wacko, Texas, in 1993. This state of mind is seemingly mad in an individual, but within the group it is accepted as a sensible consequence. The most pernicious of all belief systems, that grows up with extreme speed, is the belief that 'my' group is good, 'yours' is bad.

People are like that.

Whatever a person is confronted with and reacts to, is evaluated within a passionate good/bad dimension. And we evaluate, and are evaluated, all the time in the context of our social group. Indifferent ideas simply drop out of social existence.

It is a major transition to move from individual psychology to social psychology. The individual can hold an idea in his head without it necessarily taking a hold upon him with orgasmic fervour (though sometimes it is so). In the collective, it is almost as if there cannot be a collective that is not bound together by its idea. This especially seems so if such a collective can find another collective with a different idea – then, in a flash, 'different' becomes 'opposite'.

In fact we could go further and suggest that ideas and knowledge are social – are group behaviour. They are not just objects that an individual possesses. That is to say, ideas cannot normally be aroused to a level of conviction without the presence of someone else to confirm them. Anyone who has an idea on their own is regarded as having a bee in their bonnet, and being at least part barmy. Not so with a group of followers.

When a person comes up with an idea, he turns to others to confirm or disconfirm it. Some people are adept at getting wide agreement for the ideas they have. To some extent this is a matter of character, but also it is a matter of the social climate of opinions and of values into which his idea falls. So, it is in that context that a person has to evaluate, and in which he must form his beliefs. He must, because that is being a person. In another context that same person will have different beliefs. He has the chance of recognizing something defective in his ideas. But until he changes that cultural position he is likely to be blinkered to real criticism.

False consciousness

Ideology is the false assertion that an 'idea' is universally true. It falsifies the consciousness of other truths – the truths of other ideas. The triumphant claims for the success of market forces have been proclaimed, and partially accepted in the last decade. They have swept forward without acknowledgement that there is another 'truth': the truth that people in our society need nurture from each other, not merely bracing competition. The ideology of market forces may have *some* truth in it (about regulating people's possessiveness), but it is a partial truth. It leaves out a truth that others know (perhaps known by those with fewer possessions). Together such partial truths might create a fuller truth; apart, they drive the heady passions of group allegiances.

A false consciousness believes that it can be objective when in fact we can only see from within our own position. It leads us to judge other people's beliefs in terms of the groups we belong to. We judge their values and ideas without belonging to them and without sitting in their position. This is the false consciousness of the bourgeoisie: that it can speak, objectively, for everyone. It is also the false consciousness of a proletariat. A class consciousness is not only a partial view of the matter as a whole, it is also an indulgence in a belief that it is not a partial view; and the pretence that we can speak for everyone by taking a view from outside.

And, when the idea does spread, ideology blindfolds the awareness of why it has done so. When Christianity spread across the globe in the nineteenth century, it was not noticed that the spread resulted from military and economic conquest, not from the power of good argument, faith or the power of love. In fact such conquest resulted from superior technology which itself arose out of the dechristianizing influence of the Enlightenment. So, ironically, Christianity's success rested on non-Christian achievements. And was not noticed to do so.

Two people, in two different contexts, can evaluate and believe, not just differently, but in opposition. Then they can clash. Each will think the other is making a mistake; often attributed to malign motives in the other. Such is passion. Freud recognized this common occurrence within intergroup relations:

> it is precisely communities with adjoining territories, and related to each other in other ways as well, who are engaged in constant feuds and in ridiculing each other – like the Spaniards and the Portuguese, for instance, the North Germans and the South Germans, the English and the Scotch. I gave this phenomenon the name of 'the narcissism of minor differences', a name which does not do much to explain it ... [But by these means] cohesion between members of [each] community is made easier. (Freud, 1930, p. 114)

Inside the group it is difficult to recognize that relativity. Insight is lost. Ideas are constructs of suitable locations and these are 'group locations'. A member of a Christian church will evaluate the missions in Africa in one way, those from an Enlightenment, humanistic background, in another way. The French evaluate the fortunes of Germany in passionate terms based on the national rivalries, rather than the self-interest implicit in getting along together. The problem is not that anything goes, but that different things go, in different places, and at different times. And those differences are very specific.

Such is ideology, the falseness of our consciousness. It is a collective kind of madness, an obsession/compulsion at the crowd level.

An example of the impassioned idea

One example of this 'mistaken' assumption of good reasons is the issue of aggressive begging. This has now come up more than once in our political debates in the mid-1990s, and not with just one political party. For perhaps good reason, politicians of all shades think it is a vote-catcher.

The issue came up in its own distorted way, but was an attempt to address the reaction we might have to these dehumanized persons – the beggars. To characterize the campaign: these ne'er-do-wells who take no responsibility for themselves and their physical needs such as housing, food or gainful career, lurk in our streets; they are verbally and occasionally physically aggressive to passers-by from whom they demand the wherewithal to live which they are unwilling to find for themselves. It is possible to think of these people as simply deprived materially – hungry, cold and in ill-health. But it is more. And I think the reaction of people passing in the street is a profound anguish about the fate of a *person*. It is the fateful colleagueship with that degraded human being as well as the sympathy for their hunger which sparks a reaction in the well-fed passer-by. It is as much the destroyed person as the damaged body and its health. It is, however, that reaction to the person which is so much more difficult for us, who are more fortunate – and partly so because it is so much less articulated in our society. That was the picture presented, immediately taken up by the press, and clearly listened to with alarm and moral tutting by many normally well-meaning and charitable people. What was it that this campaign against these destroyed persons touched off in us?

As psychotherapists we know that it is very likely that what was struck was something not consciously known, yet readily active within the hearts of many people. Firstly most people, perhaps everyone, feels responsibility, and actually guilt, for suffering others. And the re-emergence of beggars so publicly in the last few years must have given rise to such feelings as these. What begging does, therefore, is directly to assault us in our more humane feelings. This allows a deft sleight of hand in the aggressive begging campaign: the suggestion that the pain of sighting beggars could be a deliberate intention on their (the beggars') part; and therefore, being so ill-intentioned, they are ruled as unworthy of feelings of guilt or charity on our part.

Those feelings of ours – guilt and responsibility – are then rendered obsolete and they must go, as it were, underground (the psychotherapist understands that this is the function of the unconscious). Feelings of guilt then resurface elsewhere – in the beggars themselves. They are responsible for causing hurt and pain to us!

Of course it is possible, with matching outrage, to counter this picture by appeal to sympathy for the vastly greater number of extremely docile, harmless and defeated beggars who exist, in reality, on our streets; or to deplore the devastating meanness of the programmes of welfare cuts which have brought all the beggars back to the streets of our towns after sixty to seventy years. In this, equally reasonable response, a specific appeal to undercurrents of passion is also being made. Those who attack beggars are themselves outrageously guilty. Guilt is being loaded back on to those attackers. Reversing the blame, by those who are outraged, is itself a method of getting out of the sense of responsibility and guilt by off-loading it into those unseemly attackers. However, piling guilt back on to those attackers meets people who have already found a means of loading their guilty feelings elsewhere – on to the beggars. They will then be driven even further, and more persistently, to find the guilt in the beggars. Or, they may find another group to burden with guilt; soon after the aggressive beggar issue was started by the Prime

Minister in 1994, Peter Lilley (the Social Services Minister) found a scandal with single mothers who had their babies simply to defraud the benefit system!

The issue of aggressive begging (and indeed single mothers) demonstrates important features. It has a reasonableness. Seemingly. However, it touches on a very different level. The level of passions. Those that concern painful guilt and responsibility in all of us. The deftness of the campaign was to render those feelings unfelt. Thus an idea, presented as a purely social issue, was in fact also a heartfelt affair of the passions. The credence given to the idea that beggars are aggressive and unworthy is evaluated by the passions. Because it gives us relief.

The features to note are (a) the seemingly straightforward political presentation, (b) the intense emotional values that are stirred by the common painful feelings (guilt and responsibility) and (c) the inability, once carried away by the passions, to see that we are in fact being so carried away. In addition, it is worth noting that the reaction to the campaign against aggressive beggars is different according to which group one belongs to – supporting the campaign if you tend to be on the right politically; and outraged by it if you tend towards the left. Your social location matters.

Position

It seems such a good idea to preserve objectivity, neutrality and reason. If only it were possible. But, despite the lure we cannot, in fact, stand on the horizon of our own world and take a distanced view. We can only start from where we are. And the lure leads us to a certainty, but a mistaken certainty, about our position. It can only be a false objectivity, a fool's gold. That is false consciousness.

That position of standing aside and apart is unattainable, for classes, for nations, for gender, for races, for sects and so on. Whatever ideas we have and impart are always driven by the moment and the place. However enduring they prove eventually to be, they arise in a context and bear its traces.

How is history made?

We like to hope that we plan rationally for our future. We develop in an orderly way. Reason dominates. Yet is that so?

I claim that social prescription and planning (social engineering) subjugate people to the good idea. It is engineering of the following ilk: collectivize the peasants, or purify Germany by eradicating non-Aryan blood. In short it is ideological. And it is disastrous.

However, even those great projects of social planning of the 1930s, German National Socialism and Soviet Communism, have eventually succumbed to unplanned history. That is an important lesson.

History is not made that way.

The transformation of society which we are at present undergoing as a result of the silicon chip and its economic exploitation was not planned. History, the development of our society, is being made under our noses. We did not prescribe that some scientist somewhere be set going to invent virtual reality.

Instead it just happened. It is true that rational scientific thinking, rational judgements and planning went into it – but into the development of the technology. The impact on society is different, not predicted, unprescribed. We watch with fascination as the technology has changed us and the world we live in. We wonder how we will live, and our children will live, next century. This is history and it is not planned in itself. What *was* planned were the gadgets that could be built, played with and exploited economically.

To put our passion behind an idea that is supposed to stand outside of, or above, society is doomed in the long run – and great heartache is involved in the course of its rise and fall. The lesson of history is, in my view, the following: we cannot trust ourselves to be reasonable and objective, we can only rely on being blinkered and obstructed by passions we can barely acknowledge.

Incidentally, beware proclamations, even of this kind! You see, even that hypothesis – that we accept the uncontrolled waywardness of passions – can itself become an idea transported into an ideology. It could support the position of extreme libertarianism (the extreme right-wing anti-state dictatorship, an example of which has been pioneered so brilliantly for decade and a half by recent Conservative governments). It proclaims the freedom to consume entirely according to one's whims and passions. And yet that idea gives rise to woeful restrictions of freedom, arising from poverty, homelessness and exploitative social relations. The ideology of libertarianism has spawned such oppression that a doomed fate for this idea is sealed. The victorious ideology of the market, which ran its course in the eighteenth and nineteenth centuries, now appears to be doing so all over again.

Searching for solutions

The problem is: what else can we do?

There are currently two competing methods for overcoming this headlong rush into a group obsession. One is to acknowledge that there is no objectivity; we are all of us in our own small worlds. This is pluralism, and it neglects the fact that pulsing undercurrents of passion intrude into reason. The other is a lofty neutrality that disdains passions, but claims a global consciousness. In fact, both are partial solutions and therefore each in its own way is fallible.

Pluralism: First, is the campaign to allow us our differences? We must legislate for that. Throughout the twentieth century one political strand of opinion has asserted democratic, egalitarian or pluralistic alternatives. They erect, self-consciously, the welfare of human beings, not ideas, as the objective of politics. Everyone should have his or her say in our multicultured, multilayered societies of the West. Minority pressure groups, single-issue politics, liberation movements create a rich mosaic of political life. But it is one which has become increasingly difficult to develop consensus in. Each small tessera is, as it were, freed from its glue. The mosaic becomes a glittering but unstable kaleidoscope. It is one in which there is a constant rubbing up against the sharp edges of someone else's obsession. Currently, we are fatefully depressed by the dominance of *this* ideology, political correctness: I cannot, as a man, have a word about women and their place in society without being disenfranchised just because I am a man – unless my words are in the form and content of women's rhetoric; I have to become as it were an honorary woman, but only by permission.

The advantages of being in one of such a 'minority' group is that it gives a full entitlement to its members to have ideas about everyone else, while mounting an intimidation against the entitlement of anyone else to have a say. Pluralism, from praiseworthy motives, can degenerate into a remarkably familiar factionalism.

Neutrality: In contrast, this is a more conservative, or patrician, stance. If there is a squabble, then the best position is to be on the fence, umpiring it. This is admirable. It has a note of conviction about it, the sensible person – sane and rational – weighing up the pros and cons: the far right or the centre right, the state versus privatization, the European currency or a federation of nation states ... Dispassionate judgement of this kind sounds the right sort of thing to bring temperance to political debate; and if only there were enough people who could create a central balance in this way we could be rescued from extremism, from the suppurating rancour between factions ... and so on.

This kind of argument against vehement political debate is common. It receives a considerable impetus from other activities in life where such neutral objectivity appears really to deliver the goods: in scientific research for instance; in the law courts; even in the proclamations of rational management in industry; and possibly in the nonjudgemental attitude of the psychotherapist faced with his patient's internal conflicts of passion. In English culture of the last hundred years (at least middle-class culture), the stiffness of the upper lip is a hallmark of resistance to the encroachments of passion upon reason. We are brought up to the resounding good sense of a neutral objectivity.

Given all this, why, then, is political debate so very far removed from this ideal? The cacophony in the House of Commons which we can now see on our televisions never reaches the sophistication of even student debates in university. There is an answer to this question. And the answer is that objective neutrality cannot be achieved, not by human beings at any rate. The nearest approximation to it is to disown one's own impassioned impulses and evaluations and see them only as the frail weaknesses of others, there to condemn them. Given the evidence of passions in political life, passionless neutrality seems a sensible goal. But neutrality is a kind of personal violence to oneself, a severing of that energy that makes us human rather than machine-like. And the result is unexpected. Reasons and passions get intermingled in ways that are uncontrolled and unconscious. Reason gets confused by unacknowledged passions; and we distract our attention from these values given by our passions through trying to (and believing we can) adopt a position of objectivity and neutrality.

Creative solutions

It is time to address the possibility of more constructive solutions. We may not be condemned to meander within this dichotomy – swayed helplessly by passions, or stiffly superior with a wooden, neutral reasonableness. Despite reservations about these contrasting mistakes, we can do nothing about the fact that human beings are passionate – however rational they might also be. One distinctive contribution that psychoanalysis has made is to understand that passion and passionate assertions of ideas are everywhere, all of the time. Not just rational assertions of them.

Therefore any exhortation to reasonableness cannot succeed unless we are familiar with, and have a vocabulary for, the throbbing of the human heart. Psychoanalysis has the materials to begin to understand those processes. But the field of operations of psychoanalysis is the heart of the individual not that of the collective. We need then to be careful about transferring our knowledge from the therapeutic setting to the social one. And the big difference is that the psychoanalyst provides himself with a carefully arranged situation in which he has some chance of keeping a part of his mind in a state in which he can reflect (as best he can) on what happens between him and his patient.

Outside that very special setting, and in the spinning confusion of ordinary social processes the psychoanalyst and psychotherapist are as lost among those currents as anyone else.

The question is: can we change our collective operation of belief systems and values so that groups, factions, classes can live together in a different way? Can we overcome the blinkered reactions to unacknowledged emotions, values, desires that are specific to location?

Recent history – this century of planning by ideas – emphasizes that no planning can avoid being ideological. But what other urge to the future can there be which is not planning by ideas? To demonstrate one instance would be to open up a chink of a possibility for finding a route around ideology, the possibility of a different kind of politics. It is enough, here, to demonstrate it is possible. We will have to leave for further work a fuller picture of what a politics of such a grouping might become.

If, currently, political groupings are welded together by the 'good idea' – about the market, about a planned economy, about fair-minded pluralism, about fundamentalism of various kinds, are there other kinds of groupings, somewhere, that are held together by something else? What sorts of collective are there which are not held by an 'idea'? And are they as malignant?

We seek something that is not necessarily rational, nor even necessarily conscious. This might be some 'thing' of the kind to which psychoanalysts could contribute, because they are more at home with the unconscious and less likely to be suspicious or scared of it.

The creative impulse: Let us consider the creative impulse. Wordsworth and Coleridge produced their *Lyrical Ballads* in 1790, as a joint enterprise. They, together with Wordsworth's sister Dorothy, formed a group that expressed very consciously their revolt against prescribed rules, and held to a belief in the pre-eminence of emotions, especially those subtle emotions evoked in the play of nature upon the senses.

Another collective identity was achieved in the early work of the cubist painters. The works of Picasso and Braque of this period are almost impossible to distinguish from each other.

They formed an identification with each other so great that their work was identical.

Neither the early romantics nor the cubists were devoid of ideas. But as collectives, they were not drawn together by their rational ideas. Instead they came together in ways which balanced their ideas with other aspects. In particular it was the urge to create.

Those collectives each changed the future of Western culture – not as a planned idea, but as a creative urge.

Possibly the most creative of all activities engaged on between human beings, is the creation of a new human life, a baby. Sex, for all its exploitability, is an impulse for the future. The family therefore represents, too, a kind of grouping based on a creative impulse.

I do not intend to go very far along this path. It is, in any case, something to be done collectively. Perhaps too, it is not very new. And indeed it might be more like an ancient footpath which has become difficult to follow because it is now so overgrown. And it is overgrown because the more inviting and well-travelled path in our culture is the rational, instrumental (especially for economic ends) and objective approach.

But I claim that these little glimmers of possibility indicate that we, human beings, can come together in collectives that are not based on ideology. It is enough to claim a new kind of political future is possible. It could, I claim, be worth exploring.

Perhaps even these movements can become 'good ideas', ones which are economically exploited. The creative urge could itself become an 'idea' and a pressing ideology as some later romantics, especially Byron, proved. It is, then, an *over*-emphasis on the pre-eminence of the sensual emotional life over reason, that overbalanced the romantic movement, the idea of passionate life. If so, it is once again a pointer to the failings that erupt from moving too far to one side or the other on the see-saw of emotions versus reason.

Initially, the creative push forward, the ones I have mentioned, relied on intuition, not reason. They were descriptive, not prescriptive. They described a state of mind or mood, they did not prescribe an ideal condition to be. Is this too the quality of a psychoanalyst's interpretation? – intuitive descriptions of a patient's narrative, rather than prescriptive instructions of his cure.

To be sure these groupings – whether cultural production or physical reproduction – can be thought about. We can have ideas about them.

Reasons and values

Let us contrast this with the process I began with. An idea is given emotional value through identifications within a social group. It is transformed by that social process into an ideology held with a consuming passion. And the passionate evaluation of rational ideas proceeds, unthinkingly, to political levels.

Now, instead of passions giving value to ideas, I think we might begin to see a possibility of rational evaluation of passions (passions which take the form, for instance, of creativity). This is to assume a different level. Clearly there is a danger that this gets into the same difficulties as the arching assumption of reasoned generalities from outside that I described earlier. However, if it is true that passions are of a moment and of a place, then rational evaluation of them could be more grounded. Such a stooping posture would therefore need to be continually worked for: reason tied to a moment.

Moreover, a level that will encompass and frame those collective evaluations, is not merely a psychology, which stands outside and looks in on people, but rather it comprises a level for addressing the collective – a political level.

This means a search for a political expression of the passionate and intuitive side of human collectives.

To be sure, political thinking must comprise the rational debate on our material and objective needs – and how they may be justly and equably supplied. But it need not be a political discourse that arouses or exploits emotional evaluations; instead we can envisage a political accounting of our emotional life and needs as well as material ones. Therefore political discourse demands a literacy of the emotions and intuitions, one which complements the discourse on our bodily needs.

Of what might a political literacy of the emotions consist?

Needs and justice: 'Man', the Bible says, 'cannot live by bread alone.' The rational provision of material bodily needs has to be augmented by the emotional provision for a person's psychological needs – in particular the need for a profound identification with a group.

Collectively we need to supply each other with more than our material needs. We have emotional needs of each other, and these needs are not merely for pleasure, but equally (perhaps more so) for the sense of being a person, and what sort of person. All our emotional needs are aroused and soothed by being a part of each other in our groups and societies. The political life of our society should attend to those psychological needs as well as to the economic supply of material ones.

Unlike material provision for each other, our emotional needs cannot be supplied under the principle of distributive justice – nor, obviously, by any kind of market. Our need to identify with a group can – should – become a political end, and not just a means of politicking.

We need our new framework to supplement collectively our emotional needs in a way that has hardly been considered in the past. When George Orwell (*Down and Out in Paris and London*) and William Henry Davies (*Autobiography of a Super-Tramp*), in the 1930s, actually joined the beggars on their travels they were involved in a political act of solidarity for the plight of tramps. It was more than just a distanced plea for better material provision and welfare. They accomplished an emotional step of going right into the lives of beggars. They identified, and survived. That solidarity of becoming is a different kind of political act. Yet it is in a sense a rather crude one. Can we not identify in ways that are reflective as well as active, while remaining genuine enough? We do not have to become a beggar in order to discover the emotional interplay within the issue of aggressive begging. Or, do we? I claim we can know – through an act of intuitive reflection, 'knowing what it feels like'. That is a political act too.

Locking into another's needs without becoming invasive, and while remaining also oneself, is an art that the psychoanalyst practices. It is a truly collective politics. The emotional needs of the human being are mediated always through others. Such needs are in fact more truly collective (and therefore political) than are the individual needs of the material body. Having, now, as a society, the wherewithal largely to supply our physical needs, we must embark on a search for a politics that can address the emotional cravings and sufferings which we so blithely relegate to personal obscurity. For the neglect of our emotional needs is at the root of the failure to provide justly for material needs

Conclusions

It is a sweeping statement to say that all social planning puts ideas above people. And yet that is the hypothesis this essay asks to be investigated further. We have to brace ourselves for a severe cultural U-turn, to seek a politics of awareness, and of description – and let fall our politics of prescription and ideological objectivity. This essay has not been, whatever else, a polemical tract on behalf of a new idea

I have wanted to experiment with a different level – one about the *way of conducting* political debate and how argument could take place. If we shift from being people with ideas, to become people who are mindful of the way we have our ideas, then we must shift from our Western view-from-the-outside stance on people. In effect, we must all be psychologists. And this book is about the way one strand of psychology, psychoanalysis and psychotherapy, can inform us about taking that new position.

As psychoanalysts and psychotherapists we do know something about our needs for emotional identifications (and distances). Group therapists and analysts know of the collective power of ideas, which are driven by hidden passions. And we have seen how political debate as it is currently conducted mingles reasons and hidden emotional values in a specific way.

A new politics has to start by unravelling that tangled knot. We must proceed by giving equal place to emotional needs and material ones. We must, finally, achieve a thoughtful container for our emotional imperatives while avoiding the relapse into a passionate espousal of proud ideas

Acknowledgement

I am deeply indebted to the stimulus of the 'Human Nature' study group which has been discussing social and political issues since 1993, when it was founded by Nicky Gavron and myself.

References

Freud, S. (1930), *Civilisation and its Discontents*, 1963; Hogarth Standard Edition, 21 S9

Commentary
IDEAS, OH DEAR!

'Beware, even of me!' says Bob Hinshelwood. In a way this sums up one of the paradoxes of this book. This is an ideas book, ideas on families, on education, on work, on politics and economics. But in this chapter Bob is saying that 'good ideas' about society pose a serious threat to us because of what we do with them. Ideas attract followers. As conviction grows among a particular group of the correctness of their ideas, these ideas become an ideology. Those who hold different ideas become the enemy. Ideas turned into ideology become the basis for social planning and social engineering, false certainties and polarization of viewpoints. We have seen this happen so many times. Ideology in economics (market forces versus welfare state), in education (self-directed discovery of a child's potential versus teaching basic skills or beliefs), in crime (understanding the criminal versus society's retribution), in health, in housing, even in psychotherapy. Indeed psychotherapy seems capable of generating a number of ideological splits all on its own, as Dorothy Rowe shows in her chapter.

What hope, then, for a chapter espousing ideas about ideology? Bob certainly tries to keep away from claiming any kind of 'good idea – follow me' line, and most of his chapter is concerned with the various snares and pitfalls along the path of trying to find a non-ideological way forward. His starting point is that there *is* no place outside political debate, so we need to tolerate and make allowance for only ever being able to have a partial view of the truth. Think of the anecdote of several people, blind or blindfolded, trying to describe an elephant from touching it. Each describes a different part, the leg, the trunk, the tusk, the belly. Each thinks he is describing the truth which is, of course, different from what each of the others describes. Well, imagine that we, collectively, make up the elephant. Each of us somewhere in its large mass. What we can see depends entirely on where we are. This is Bob's point about location Where you are socially, politically, culturally, shapes and limits what you see.

If we are seeking universal truth this is bad news. On the other hand, if we *accept* that our vision is limited, our truths partial and more than likely to be mistaken in some respects, this is better, Bob argues, than the 'false consciousness' of thinking we really do have an overview of human society. If recognizing that you are likely to be mistaken doesn't sound much, can you imagine how different the course of history would have been if this had been a priority for most political and religious leaders?

One of the problems with ideology is that it forms the basis for social planning and social engineering on a grand scale. Bob's argument is that such planning is doomed, that history is simply not made that way. He gives the enormous impact of the silicon chip as an example of unplanned history. The artist David Hockney, in an interview for Yorkshire television in 1996, commented on the unexpected historical importance of the Xerox machine, which enables information to be easily and widely distributed by individuals or small groups. The attempt in some countries to ban private ownership of photocopiers was in Hockney's view an indication that the regimes in these countries would not last long in their attempt to halt the tide of history. Perhaps the most significant aspect of the Internet is not to link up myriad interest groups in the affluent West but to put another nail in the coffin of attempts by social planners to maintain power by control of information across national boundaries.

If ideology is disastrous, and doesn't work in the end, we should avoid it. Bob points out that this is easier said than done. He warns us against accepting ways of overcoming the dangers of ideology that are themselves flawed. Pluralism sets out to give all groups and cultures an equal voice but ends up with a different kind of tyranny, with any group claiming the right to express its views including those which may be harmful to others. Limiting the risks of pluralism brings us back to the problem of asserting one ideology over others.

Objective neutrality is also a false trail, because it denies the existence of passion, leading to political debate which has the appearance of being logical while pushing under the carpet – preferably someone else's carpet – uncomfortable awareness of responsibility and guilt or shame. Bob gives the detailed example of aggressive begging, but when it comes to blaming others we could be forgiven for thinking that pass the (guilt) parcel was the only game in town in British political life. In 1996 British government ministers tried to portray as irrational anyone anxious that BSE or 'mad cow disease' might get into the human food chain and pose a threat to human life, an anxiety that led to a near worldwide ban on British beef. By seeking to portray this anxiety as irrational, they partly succeeded in keeping attention away from their own guilt in failing to monitor what was going into animal food since 1988 (when the disease became notifiable) while claiming in public that everything necessary was being done. The government presented itself as objective and scientific and others – in this case foreigners – as unreasonable. Reason and emotion were separated and brought into opposition.

People are like that, says Bob. Has he led us to an impasse? Ideology is poisonous, but the main remedies don't work. As social creatures we need something to bind us together with our group. The isolated existence is not available. That bond has usually been one sort of ideology or another. What Bob very tentatively suggests is that the creative impulse may provide the basis for social bonds that do not involve ideology. He writes about very small groups of painters and poets. Is this fanciful? It brought to mind the experience of one of us (D.K.) as an aspiring saxophone player in jazz and blues bands in the 1960s. Improvising music together could be the next best thing to making love, producing a sense of immersion and intimacy, as well as periods of tension and conflict. Alan Parker's film *The Commitments* portrays this mixture beautifully and movingly. Being part of a shared creative activity is arguably one of the most enriching experiences available to human beings. Other groups of creatively connected people – actors, dancers, football teams – share these close bonds which are free of ideology (although ideology is never far away as when conflict arises over the purity of artistic values versus the potential for economic exploitation). Could such creative groups and couplings be the basis for a non-ideological society? Could sexual relationships be rescued from the layers of glamorization and exploitation that have been wrapped around them and be a source of creative non-ideological fulfilment at least for part of our lives? From where we stand it is hard to imagine how society could operate along these lines, but what impact would it have if everyone was able to be part of a creative collective for some of the time or for a period of their lives? Such a suggestion sits alongside those of other contributors to this book looking for new approaches to living together.

In working with their clients, psychotherapists and counsellors recognize it as a sign of progress when the client can begin to loosen their grip on absolutist thinking, on ideas that are asserted as universally true, and admit the possibility of gradations between black and white, of uncertainty. 'No one likes me' becomes 'I recognize I can upset people by some of the things I say.' 'I'm a total failure' becomes 'I make mistakes sometimes but I can live with that, I don't have to be perfect.' As Bob says, individuals can be good losers, groups seldom are. The question his chapter asks is can we begin to develop groups – creative, political, work-based – that have the capacity to tolerate the uncertainty of knowing they don't have all the answers?

Chapter 8
THE COMFORTS OF UNREASON
Dorothy Rowe

In my salad days when I was green in judgement I believed that universal enlightenment was possible. I saw that the body of human stupidity far outweighed the body of human knowledge and wisdom with the result that just about all of the vastness of human suffering derived not from natural causes but from what we do to one another and to ourselves. However, I believed that the forces of unreason (the kind of thinking which results when fear, greed, vanity and the desire for power are allowed to prevail over logic and scientific thinking) could be exposed for what they were and thus defeated. I thought that psychotherapy would be the means by which this would happen. Through psychotherapy we would come to understand that all we know is what we have constructed, and that out of this understanding we would develop new ways of living together based on tolerance, mutual dignity and knowledge informed by the search for truth rather than the fulfilment of desires.

Now I know that this has not occurred and might never occur. I no longer see psychotherapy as being as profound as I once thought it was. Moreover, the forces of unreason are not so easily routed, and, when they do suffer a defeat in some area of experience the forces quickly regroup and capture other territory. This happens because not only do these forces serve to keep power in the hands of those who would be powerful (in political thought such people are usually grouped together as the Church and the State, those organizations which determine through education and censorship what their citizens should know[1]) but they often secretly subvert those who believe that they are in the vanguard of enlightenment. Enlightenment requires a person to look with clear, unwavering eyes at the reality of our existence, but, as T. S. Eliot said, 'Human kind cannot bear very much reality.'[2]

When reality becomes too much to bear we can comfort ourselves with fantasies, which is wise provided we remember that the stories we tell ourselves are fantasies. If we fail to do this, if we think that our fantasies are real and true, we join the forces of unreason. In the ranks of therapists there are some who do just this. They develop a logic which conveniently ignores those constructions which do not fit their theories and thus they collude with the forces of unreason. Therapists whose model of therapy includes terms like transpersonal, spirituality, the soul, the religious, the transcendent, the numinosum, the sacred are prone to do this. Freud ignored much of the actual brutality which his clients had suffered and many of his disciples over the following decades have done the same.[3]

Such collusion seems on many occasions to go beyond a mere failure of nerve. It seems instead to be an inability to understand and accept the peculiarity of our existence.

This peculiarity is that, while the world we live in seems to be solid and real and shared with others, what we each experience is our individual construction. We can imagine events which occur without any relationship to us, but what we have is not knowledge about such events but theories about such events. In

151

fact, everything we know is a theory, a construction, and this construction is inside our head.

When I lecture about this I often quote or refer to the work of the scientist Ian Stewart when he wrote,

> The problem is that human beings cannot obtain an objective view of the universe. Everything we experience is mediated by our brains. Even our vivid impression that the world is 'out there' is a wonderful trick. The nerve cells in our brains create a simplified copy of reality inside our head, and then persuade us that we are inside it, rather than the other way around.[4]

I then describe how, while it seems to me that I am here and my audience over there, actually what I am experiencing is inside my head. I can only hope that whatever is going on around me bears some resemblance to my construction. I go on to say that the same process is occurring in each person present, and that if it were possible to take our pictures out of our heads like a photograph out of a Polaroid camera, hang them on the wall and look at them we would see that each picture is different from all the others.

This is because our construction can come from nowhere other than our past experience, and no two people, not even identical twins, have the same experience.

As I describe this basic physiological process I watch the expressions on the faces of my audience. Some people look mildly interested, unsurprised because I am not telling them anything they do not know, but others, often people who would regard themselves as well educated, look confused, even anxious. They have never heard such an account of experience before.

In a workshop which I was running for some Australian psychologists and social workers and where I had given this account of how we create meaning, one young woman said, 'I am a committed Christian and I know that people are born bad.' A little further in the discussion another woman said, 'There's no doubt that depression can be caused by biological changes.' Both these statements reveal an ignorance of how we are, in essence, meaning-creating creatures.

The first speaker, like many theologians and philosophers, claimed to have a super-human access to the Absolute Truth, that is, a Truth which exists eternally outside time and space and human experience but which can be accessed by a special few. (Plato saw an élite of philosophers having such an access, while being inducted into the priesthood is in essence being given special access to God's power.[5]) This would be believable if Absolute Truths were rare and consistent with one another but there seem to be as many Absolute Truths as there are people claiming to be special. Such Absolute Truths are far from consistent.

The second speaker had failed to read with a psychologist's critical eye the research literature on the search for a biological basis for depression and had not realized that it is not bodily changes which determine our thoughts, feelings and actions but how we interpret our bodily changes. (To understand this it is necessary to remember that awareness and interpretation are simultaneous and that an interpretation need not be conscious for us to act on it.) A burst of adrenaline can be interpreted as fear or pleasurable excitement. A change in serotonin levels might be interpreted as, 'I don't feel well. I'm going to take it easy. Someone else can do my work', or, 'I don't feel well. This is my punishment for being so wicked. Everything is hopeless.' (This second example is pure speculation as changes in serotonin levels or any other biochemical change have not been shown to precede depression.)

Because all that we have are our interpretations, we are free to choose to acknowledge that what we have are theories and that we can use all means to test these theories (George Kelly, ever hopeful, spoke of 'man the scientist'[6]), or we can insist that our theories are not theories but accurate representations of the truth.

Of course, acknowledging that all you know is a theory which might or might not approximate to reality requires the courage to live with uncertainty, and many people (some therapists included) lack such courage. It also requires courage to acknowledge that the theories we form do not range over the infinity of possible constructions but they are themselves determined by what can be said in the framework. For instance, each of the world's languages is a theory about the nature of reality. If you speak English you can construct theories only in terms of what English allows you to construct. Many of the most fruitless enterprises of psychologists and psychiatrists have stemmed from the failure to see how the English language prefers nouns to verbs, thus rendering it prone to reification, especially when its users believe that if there is a word there must be an object to which that word refers. Hence the futile search for imaginary things like 'intelligence', 'personality', 'depression' and 'schizophrenia'.

The failure to recognize that what can be said is determined by the framework of such constructions is not confined to psychologists and psychiatrists. Those who would be powerful and those who prefer fantasy to reality often fail to acknowledge or even understand that this is so. Thus a grocer's daughter can proclaim that value for money is a universal principle, and a devout Christian surviving a near-death experience does not see Shiva at the end of the tunnel into the next world.

What is this inability to accept and acknowledge the peculiarity of our existence? Over the past twenty years I have taught – or tried to teach – about this to a wide range of people, differing in nationality, culture, religion, class and education. I have found that some people have no difficulty in understanding the peculiarity of their existence while others remain baffled and confused or dismiss out of hand what I say. These responses do not relate to the person's level of education. Indeed, I feel that a tertiary education (or what passes as a tertiary education) is actually an impediment to understanding.

Most of the nuclear physicists I have encountered find what I say blindingly obvious. After all, physicists have been dealing with this issue in their science since the 1920s. It is other scientists who want to believe that somehow in doing science they step outside themselves, don the white coat of objectivity and perceive reality directly. They find the thought that they cannot measure anything absolutely accurately unacceptable. Many such scientists are psychologists.

Teaching psychologists and highly qualified psychotherapists I find the hardest chore of all. Many of them come with a set of mental boxes which they call psychological theories. As I talk I see what I am saying being popped into one of the boxes and the lid snapped tight. To pass examinations in psychology and psychotherapy you have to know the current theories and their accepted refutation – or supposed refutation because more times than not the refutation of a theory is no more than name-calling, and there is nothing well-trained psychologists like better than polysyllabic abstract nouns. Such words can allow the user to ignore experience, especially those experiences which challenge the psychologist's favourite theory.

Of course highly educated psychologists and psychotherapists are not the only people who pop everything they encounter into a theory box and snap the lid shut tight. Listen to the pundits on Radio Four's *The Moral Maze* and you will hear them doing the same. Thus lived experience is ignored and what is enjoyed is the comfort of prejudice. As Freud once observed, intellectualization is the most reliable of the defences.

Is this inability to acknowledge and accept the peculiarity of our existence more than a result of an education aimed at moulding docile citizens rather than enlightening individuals? After all, it is never in the interests of the Church and the State to have their claims to possession of the Absolute Truth challenged in any way. As small children we are well aware that our way of seeing things is very different from that of our parents, but unfortunately for most of us we are not allowed to hold on to such an understanding. Instead we are told that our individual truths are silly, childish, wrong, wicked. If we accept such teaching and grow up believing that there is just one right way of thinking, feeling and acting we lead miserable lives because we have lost the one freedom which makes our life survivable, even happy and glorious. Such freedom comes from understanding that though we can control very little of the circumstances of our life we are always free to change how we interpret those circumstances.

The turning point in psychotherapy, so I have observed, is the moment when the person actually reaches such an understanding. This is an understanding which the person now knows through and through. It saturates and transforms the person's entire structure of meaning. If the person has only an intellectual grasp of this understanding then nothing is gained. Unfortunately there are many psychotherapists of different theoretical persuasions who pay lip-service to such an understanding but who imply in their interchanges with their clients that they are in possession of some Absolute Truth which, in time, they will disclose to the client.

Thus are those psychotherapists who want to be powerful seduced by the forces of unreason. The desire to be powerful reveals itself in many ways. It may be that the psychotherapist wants to secure a good income, or become famous, or simply assure himself of his self-worth by making his clients better. But as long as the psychotherapist is saying to the client, 'I know best. Do it my way,' the psychotherapist has yielded to the forces of unreason.

Hence psychotherapy has not transformed the world. Far too many psychotherapists have been seduced in this way. Such psychotherapists can be found in all schools of therapy, even in Personal Construct Psychology. Psychoanalysts were seduced right from the start.

When I was doing my diploma in clinical psychology at the University of Sydney in 1964 we studied in great detail Otto Fenichel's *Psychoanalytic Theory of the Neuroses*. I found the book fascinating. All my family and friends were in it as well as myself and it explained so much. I learned the jargon and tried not to be too discomforted by the way Otto talked down to me, implying that he and his fellow psychoanalysts not only possessed the True Knowledge but they were wise and wonderful people leading wise and wonderful lives. Certainly the psychologists and psychiatrists I knew who worked in a psychoanalytic framework were far from being wise and wonderful but they were mere Australians. What would they know?

In 1968 I arrived in England alarmed and excited by the prospect of meeting those wise and wonderful psychoanalysts who, unlike me, had life sussed out. I actually made a pilgrimage to see Joseph Sandler to ask if it would be all right to use Kelly's theory and techniques in my research. He said that it would.

Joseph Sandler was kind, as many psychoanalysts are, and from what I knew of him an admirable person. Now I know many Freudians, Jungians and Lacanians, some strict adherents to their faith, others liberal in their views. Some are eminently likeable and some decidedly strange. None, fortunately, has proved to be as power-mad as Freud or Melanie Klein, whose relationships with those who did not agree with them does not provide an edifying spectacle. But, alas, not one of these psychoanalysts has proved to be a wise and wonderful person who has really sussed life out. They manage their lives no better nor worse than do the rest of us.

Not that this prevents many of them from talking down to the ignorant unanalysed. They believe that they are in possession of the Absolute Truth and so they can enjoy the comforts of unreason.

Unreason seeks to satisfy desires and to do so must frustrate the search for what is. Science seeks to establish what is, irrespective of our desires. Psychotherapy has not transformed and enlightened the world or even a small part of it because in seeking to understand ourselves we fail to be scientific. As the renowned naturalist Edward O. Wilson said:

> To me it is remarkable that we do not live in a scientific age, as much as we might think otherwise. We live in an age in which we are – at least people in developed countries are – benefiting from remarkable advances in science and technology, but in our thinking, in our linguistic expression, in our way in which we deal with the universe intellectually, we are still prescientific. We might as well be agriculturalists in the Fertile Crescent, in terms of how we combine scientific knowledge with our daily idioms of thought, and I think that one of the great challenges, intellectually and in the immediate future, is to find a way of combining the best in scientific knowledge and thinking and concept and creativity, with the best of the humanities, and develop a scientific culture.[7]

The scientific culture of which Wilson speaks would be one which takes as its starting point the recognition that from some point in our gestation to our death, asleep or awake, conscious or unconscious, drunk or sober, in thinking, feeling and doing, each of us is creating meaning. Meaning is our being. We have nothing else other than the meaning we create.

Such an understanding should be the basis of psychology and psychotherapy. But it is not. Back in the 1960s an American psychologist called Rosenthal published his research which showed that if teachers thought certain children were intelligent the children behaved intelligently, that test results differed according to the gender of the researchers and of the subjects, and that psychologists got the results they expected even when the subjects were rats. In short, he showed that it is not what happens to us which determines what we think, feel and do but how we interpret what happens to us (Rosenthal and Jacobson, 1968). I remember a friend, a lecturer at Sydney University, seeking to dismiss Rosenthal, saying, 'If his results are only half way accurate we'll have to do every experiment over again.' I thought that she was right and that psychologists should start again. But they did not. Status, as ever, was more important than truth.

It would be possible to construct a psychology and psychotherapy based on the knowledge that we construct what we know. Here we would recognize that emotion is not separate from cognition but is, as is our construction of metaphor and image, a way of creating meaning. We would understand that communication is not a matter of passing something (a communication, a thought, a feeling) from one person to another but a process of individual interpretations, full of opportunities for mutual misunderstandings. We would elaborate the methods of science in the testing of our personal, political, artistic and scientific theories. We would search for shared patterns of constructions and delineate the amazing variations of individual constructions. In all we would celebrate the creativity of our inventions for we would know that if there were one fixed reality and that was what each of us saw how dreary our lives would be.

If only we would do this.

Must the meagre vanities of cowardice and the desire for power always prevail?

Notes

1. For a full discussion of this see Dorothy Rowe (1991).
2. 'Burnt Norton', *Four Quartets*, Faber, 1974, p. 20.
3. See the discussion of Freud's 'Infantile Mental Life: Two Lies Told by Children', in Dorothy Rowe (1994), pp. 123–7.
4. *Guardian*, 19 June 1992.
5. In the Church of England the chief argument against women being admitted to the priesthood is that women are incapable of coping with or are unworthy of the magical powers which enable the priest to act in God's name.

   Edward de Bono (*Guardian*, 3 September 1994) gave a succinct account of Plato's views. Plato believed that just as Pythagoras had demonstrated ultimate truths in mathematics so there should be ultimate truths everywhere ... Plato could not abide the messy relativism of the Sophists – many of whom were modern system thinkers – because they were doctors, and as such knew that a substance given at one stage in an illness was beneficial but given at another stage was dangerous. Similarly, the right amount was curative and a larger amount could be fatal. So whether something was 'good' or 'bad' depended on the circumstance and the system.

   Plato and, later, Christian thinkers knew that the world could not be run on such relativistic lines. Plato's *Republic* suggests a Utopia in which there is no voting but a scientific breeding of rulers. There are no families but government crèches instead. Not surprisingly, the Nazi party had as their official doctrine the productions of 'guardians' as specified by Plato.
6. George Kelly was the creator of Personal Construct Psychology. See, for example, Kelly (1963). A good introduction to his work is Bannister and Fransella (1968).
7. *Guardian*, 31 August 1995.

References

Bannister, D. & Fransella, F. (1986), *Inquiring Man*, Croom Helm
Fenichel, O. (1963), *Psychoanalytic Theory of the Neuroses*, Croom Helm
Kelly, G. (1963), *A Theory of Personality*, Norton
Rosenthal, R. & Jacobson, L. (1986), *Pygmalion in the Classroom: Teacher Expectations and Pupils' Intellectual Development*. Holt, Rinehart & Winston
Rowe, D. (1991), *Wanting Everything*, HarperCollins
– (1994), *Time on Our Side*, HarperCollins

Commentary
COLD COMFORT

Unlike our other contributors Dorothy Rowe sees psychotherapy, or at least most psychotherapists, as obstacles to the search for new meanings and autonomy. Psychotherapists and counsellors are part of the power structure of vested interests, whether they know it or not. Rather than get caught up in defending psychotherapy, we would say that this is an issue psychotherapists are now very alive to. Dorothy's critique of psychoanalysis certainly would carry force if directed at its early decades, when there were acrimonious power struggles and ideological conflicts between different factions. But psychoanalysts have also led the way in recognizing the need for therapists to refrain from imposing their own views on the client. Bion, the distinguished post-war British psychoanalyst, advocated that the psychotherapist should rid himself of 'all memory and desire' in working with patients – that is, of any wish to influence the patient towards the therapist's desired goals (Bion, 1967). He would agree with the risk of wanting the patient to 'do it the therapist's way'. Foulkes, a psychoanalyst who became the founder of Group Analysis, wrote that the leader in such groups 'must have outgrown and be immune against the temptation, however strong, to play God and to use his group for his own satisfaction' (Foulkes, 1964, pp. 64–5). These therapists, two of the most influential in Britain in the last thirty years, knew the risks and knew the responsibilities.

Dorothy argues that many psychotherapists followed Freud in ignoring the actual brutality experienced by his patients. This is now well recognized, and psychotherapists are far more inclined to support their patients in coming to terms with what really happened in their lives. The suggestion that although we cannot control much of our circumstances we are free to change how we interpret them is two-edged. It *could* be taken as a recipe for passivity and fatalism. Be happy. Accept your lot. Adjust yourself, not society. Or it *could* be a basis for feeling empowered to do something. You may have been victimized, but you don't have to *be* a victim. Life may be full of misfortune, but there are always opportunities if you can view your situation in terms of the difference you can make. It may be no more than the escape into fantasy from a horrific present. It may be redefining your identity as a self-employed person after years of being a 'company' person. It may be forming a political pressure group, or discovering your creativity in some form. Isn't this what this whole book is about? Changing the meaning of events can empower us to do something, not be victims.

Dorothy describes how she started off having high expectations of what psychotherapy could achieve – and was disappointed. It may be that many of psychotherapy's critics, especially those who once believed strongly in its power for good, criticize for similar reasons – they feel let down that it doesn't have all the answers. It is interesting to contrast what Dorothy expected from the way another contributor to this book, Bob Hinshelwood, suggests psychotherapy can be helpful, for they seem to have almost opposite expectations. Dorothy thought psychotherapy would replace a way of living together based on irrational forces with a way based on knowledge, informed by the search for truth, and based on scientific rationality. Bob suggests that our mistake is that we assume our knowledge *can be* based on neutral objectivity. For him psychotherapy helps us see that our ideas are always influenced by what Dorothy might call the forces of unreason. Knowing this can at least help us be aware of our tendency to get it wrong when we think we've got it right. A lower expectation, but perhaps one we can do more with.

Dorothy reminds us that psychotherapists who think they are 'in the vanguard of enlightenment' may nevertheless be subverted by their own greed, fear or wish for power. They are not immune, that is for sure. But then no one is. No one can step outside their world and view it in a completely detached way, much as we might try and much as some might claim so to do. Realizing this can lead to angry despair, to a live-for-today-someone's-got-to-win-the-lottery attitude, or to a tentative move forward into an uncertain future, using our awareness of the risks to guide us where possible.

We cannot know our world objectively because we are inside it. Dorothy and Bob both argue for the acceptance of uncertainty, a willingness to accept our fallibility and proneness to mistakes. The shift away from certainty – scary and potentially invigorating – may be exciting for those who have enough inner strength to deal with the chaos in the world. But most of us, in letting go of our certainties, need to feel 'held' by something.

A student counsellor described a client, a young man with an authoritarian father who had had several goes at deciding on a career. He had tried his hand at music and drama but his performances were unreliable. So were his friendships. He had little sense of permanence or direction. The attraction of temporary forgetfulness via alcohol and drugs was irresistible. He longed for an ideology to hang on to, a set of rules, beliefs, a 'containing philosophy'.

Many clients of psychotherapists and counsellors present a similar need. Their need may be so great that they risk becoming converted to and taken over by any ideology that offers the illusion of complete reassurance. Hence Dorothy's deep concerns about psychotherapists who are willing to offer this. Resisting the lure of easy answers, of a formula, an ideology, a grand theory, while searching for something to hold on to as a foundation for our sense of identity and belonging, is at the very heart of what this book is trying to do.

References

Bion, W. R. (1967), 'Notes on Memory and Desire', *Psycho-analytic Forum*, vol. II (3)
Foulkes, S. H. (1964), *Therapeutic Group Analysis*, George Allen & Unwin

Chapter 9
THE ECONOMIC PSYCHE: TOWARDS A POLITICS OF TRANSFORMATION
Andrew Samuels

The politics of transformation

Politics in the West is experiencing some important and difficult changes: old definitions, assumptions and values are being transformed. Politics will always be about struggles for power and the control of resources, but a new understanding of the function of politics in our lives has evolved since feminism introduced the phrase 'the personal is political'.

The new kind of politics is often on a feeling level, involving a politics of subjectivity, that encompasses a key interplay between public and private dimensions of power. Since feminism, we recognize that political power is not just manifested in governments and those who oppose or challenge them. Political power is insidious, found in family organization, gender and race relations, connections between wealth and health, control of information, and in philosophy, religion and art.

Few would disagree that, in all these senses, politics in Western countries is in a mess. We urgently need fresh ideas and approaches. Positive political energy has certainly left the political parties and the old, formal political system. (Political energy at its best means the capacity to bring imagination, creativity and effort to bear on seemingly intractable problems in the attempt to solve them in ways that reflect concern for social justice.) Yet formal politics has still got the resources and most of the decisions will in the future still be taken via the electoral system. This state of affairs is not merely depressing, it is schizoid because political energy has moved on into a plethora of seemingly unconnected social movements: environmentalism, feminism, consumerism, ethnopolitics, human and animal rights movements, liberation theology and so on.

The growth of these social and cultural movements has been a striking feature of the past twenty years in modern societies like Britain and the United States. They have become a leading form of social life for many. More and more people are involved in such networks – increasingly aware that what they are doing may be regarded as political. The elasticity in our idea of politics is not something done to it by intellectuals. It is rather something politics seems actively to embrace. These new social movements operate in isolation from each other and apparently have quite different agendas and programmes. Yet their collective impact, if it could be garnered without damaging the spontaneity and creativity of what is going on in the various groups, may be just what Western societies need as we stumble towards the end of the century.

What these disparate social movements have in common is their psychological similarity. They share in an emotional rejection of 'big' politics with its pomposity and self-interest, its mendacity and complacency. They share a common philosophy (or set of values) that is based on ideas of living an intelligible and purposeful life in spite of the massive social forces that mitigate against intelligibility and purpose. From this commitment to values comes a disgust with present politics and politicians. Sometimes people talking about our official political structure report a quite physical disgust, the gagging reflex, an ancient part of the nervous system, absolutely necessary for survival in a world full of literal and metaphorical toxins.

What is going on is the frank pursuit of a transformation of the political process. I have chosen to call this an attempt at the resacralization of politics. The aim is to get back into political culture a sense of purpose, decency, aspiration, and even holiness. Even if such a state of affairs never really existed in the past, most of us tend to behave as though there were a time when it did – hence *re*sacralization.

A commonly raised issue in Western political commentary these days is how to translate our emotional, bodily and imaginative responses – to Bosnia, ecological disaster, homelessness, unemployment, poverty worldwide – into action. Is there any way that we can make political use of our private reactions to public events? There is a sense in which this is a core political problem of our times: how we might convert passionately held political convictions – shall we call them political dreams? – into practical realities.

Perhaps we need to rethink what we expect a citizen to be, shifting our assumptions in the direction of the 'psychological citizen' (to use a term developed independently by James Hillman, 1992, and myself). This citizen is a 'politically self-aware' citizen, knowing already that the personal, inner and private levels of life connect up with the political, outer and public levels. But the culture in which she or he lives is very reluctant to make this connection. Its reluctance is in a way surprising because people have always spoken about politics and politicians in terms that are emotional such as 'character'. And a good deal of political debate boils down to disagreement about what is human nature (what deters a criminal, or inspires someone to support herself, or motivates citizens in an economic sense).

Perhaps we should get more used to the fact that we now talk a mixed language of psychology *and* politics. This language serves a political-psychological hybrid. In it, we will have to know not only what is being said, but who is saying it – and maybe even which part of a person is talking. Everyone notoriously teems with inner people ('sub-personalities') from vulnerable inner child to Wise Old Man and this is always a difficult thing to acknowledge in discourse. We need to further an approach to politics that understands that no society has a single, unified identity either. In our divided and divisive culture, politics and pluralistic questions of psychological roles and identities seem to be linked as never before. This is because of myriad other interminglings: ethnic, socio-economic, national. The picture is made more dense by events in the realms of gender and sexuality.

How does the psychological citizen grow and develop? The individual person lives not only her or his life but also the life of the times. Jung told his students that 'when you treat the individual you treat the culture'. Even persons keen to differentiate themselves cannot be seen in isolation from the society and culture that have played a part in forming them. Once we see that there is a political person who has been evolving over time, we will want to track the political history of that person – starting with the way the political events of her or his lifetime have impacted on the forming of a personality that may or may not grow beyond these events to achieve a sense of political agency. We have to consider the politics a person has inherited from their family, class, ethnic, religious, national background – not forgetting the crucial choices that sex and sexual orientation impose. Nor can we neglect what we have learned from Freud about reaction formation and from Jung about compensation – sometimes people take on their parents' politics; equally often, people reject what their parents stood for.

There is an interesting relationship of class and the inner world. Many people in the West have achieved a higher socio-economic status than that of their parents. And yet, in the inner world, the social class in which they function is often the social class into which they were born. There is a psychological tension that exists within the socially and economically mobile citizen between what he or she is and what he or she was. I think this tendency brings with it an interesting message for a progressive political and social project. To the extent that the typical move is from traditional working class to middle class, and to the extent that a collective passion (and need) for social and economic justice does still exist in the working class, it is possible to identify within some socially mobile middle-class individuals who seek psychotherapy a residual concern for economic and social justice, still appropriate to their inner world location of self as working class and oppressed.

But this account of political psychology is perhaps over-rational. If there is something inherently political in humans, then maybe the politics a person has cannot only be explained by social inheritance. Maybe there is an accidental, constitutional, fateful and inexplicable element to think about. For instance, people may be born with different amounts and types of political energy in them.

If that is so, then there would be big implications, both for these individuals and for their approach to politics. What happens when a person with a high level of political energy is born to parents with a low level of it (or vice versa)? What if the two parents have vastly different levels from each other? What is the fate of a person with a high level of political energy born into an age and a culture which does not value such a high level, preferring to reward lower levels of political energy? The answers to such questions shape not only the political person but the shape and flavour of the political scene in their times.

The questions continue on a more personal level. Did your parents foster or hinder the flowering of your political energy and your political potential? How did you develop the politics you have at this moment? In which direction are your politics moving – and why? I do not think these questions are presently on either a mainstream or an alternative political agenda.

My interest is not in what might be called political maturity. I doubt that such a universal exists as the widely skewed evaluation, by different commentators, of the 'terrorists' others call 'freedom fighters' show. My interest is in how people got to where they are politically; in how they themselves think, feel, explain and communicate about that process of arrival, so that I prefer to speak of the political myth of the person. From a psychological angle, it often turns out that people are not actually where they thought they were politically, or that they got there by a route they did not know about.

An awareness that politics is psychological is the theme that links all engaged in the multiple present-day discussions about the loss of meaning, purpose and responsibility to each other in communal and personal life. Such is the Western fear of the inner world, however, that its implications for political life are barely recognized, let alone discussed or made use of. I am thinking of the ways in which persons are connected in the inner world that do not rest on exclusively social or communal realities. It is tragic how little discussion there has been about the radical, socialized, transpersonal psychology that is needed to make visions of community and communitarian politics less oppressive in their appeal to traditional social forms. But there are psychological theories in existence that focus on the transpersonal ways in which people are already linked and attuned to one another, already living in psychological connection in a social ether. In this story about humanity, it is possible to learn that we were never as separate from each other as so-called free market, neo-liberal politics claimed us to be. The kinds of pre-existing connections between people, which politicians and citizens urgently need to explore and cultivate, may be largely non-verbal, working on a transpersonal psyche-to-psyche level. We could see ourselves as stalks growing, feeding and flowering from the same underground rhizome. Unfortunately, as the history of its development shows, psychoanalysis has never been quite comfortable with theories of shared psychological states, missing the radical potential of a socialized, transpersonal psychology. Psychoanalysis has castigated such states as 'mystical' or 'ecstatic' or 'oceanic' (with nothing favourable being meant by these words), or has tended to see them as relevant only to crowd psychology or to an understanding of the psychology of fascism.

Psychotherapy and politics

Many attempts to link psychology and politics have been academic, involving empirical work on such things as voting patterns or the birth order of political leaders. More ambitious applications of psychoanalytic and Jungian ideas have ended up as mechanical and from on-high, providing us with simplistic solutions to very complicated political problems. The hidden agenda of many of these psychoanalytic and Jungian explorations of politics has mostly been to prove the psychological theories of the thinker right and this may be a reason for the lack of acceptance by political theorists and activists.

Without resorting to the empirical research route or to the route that displays the dogmatism and self-referentiality of some psychoanalysts and Jungians, I have been trying for some time to present an approach to modern politics that makes use of what we learn about politics in the outer world from ordinary clinical practice in psychotherapy (Samuels, 1993). These explorations of our hidden politics may start with the ideas and methods of therapy but take them well away from the clinical office, out into the streets and cities, the mountains and forests, the families and organizations, and especially into the world of economics and finance whose politics have become dulled and monochrome.

What might the role of psychology and the psychotherapies be in a transformed politics, based on a search for intelligibility and purpose in social life, a search that is implicitly and sometimes explicitly transpersonal and spiritual in tone? We must first acknowledge the limitations of a psychological approach to politics. Freud, Jung and the founders of humanistic psychology like Maslow had ambitions to be of use in the political world. There have been two main responses to such ambitions. First, the world never really showed up for its first therapy session with them! I do not think this reluctance by twentieth-century politics to undergo psychological treatment of itself can all be put down to resistance to therapists. There is something offensive and ridiculous about the mechanical psychological reductionism that has been produced from time to time. I recall an article by a psychoanalyst in a newspaper about the phallic symbolism of cruise missiles going down ventilator shafts in Baghdad, and a statement by another analyst that students protesting in Paris in 1968 were functioning as a 'regressive' group. He didn't say how he would have recognized a progressive group. Jungians are just as bad: it doesn't help to be told that the military-industrial complex is all due to the Greek god Hephaestus. So-called archetypal themes and images can get used just as reductively as any Freudian idea that childhood is decisive. Both are equally problematic in politics. Both schools have as a major goal the attempt to prove their theories right. Similarly, arguments that all will be well were we to access a wholly different dimension of life ('soul') will justifiably be dismissed by politicians and social scientists alike as simplistic and one-dimensional.

The second response has been an appropriation of psychological theory in the service of hegemonistic and totalizing political projects. As Sonu Shamdasani has pointed out (personal communication, 1995), we should bear in mind the careful reading of Le Bon by Mussolini and Hitler, the military development of intelligence testing in the First World War, and even the links between cognitive psychology and Star Wars. On this reading, psychology and psychoanalysis have been far too politicized, with often appalling consequences.

Both these responses take psychology and psychoanalysis in isolation. The psychoanalytic and Jungian commentators on politics inflate their expertise and their claims, sometimes seeming to deny social and other material realities. The dictators or generals making use of psychology clearly saw it as a useful and effective tool (which it is) but did not care to relate its instrumental effectiveness to the liberal and humane values that underpin it. In the present-day context, while it would be impossible to say that such dangers could be got rid of altogether, it is possible to temper them by suggesting and even insisting that psychoanalysis and Jungian psychology be applied to public and policy issues always and only in a multidisciplinary way. One image that captures this is to envision a situation in which an analyst or therapist sits on relevant policy-forming committees as part of a spectrum of 'experts'. Just as a committee might have a statistician or economist, so too it might have an analyst or therapist sitting on it.

A multidisciplinary approach is also crucial in facing a third, more contemporary possibility that something central to politics might be lost if political psychology is left in isolation as the preserve of the media and its political pundits. It is not that the columnists or presenters ignore psychology altogether. They certainly use a form of psychology. My concern is that a false dialogue has been started between psychology and the politicians in which we all join in a wild analysis of our politicians in a desperate search for the one with personal stability and integrity.

Therapists can contribute what their clients tell them to multidisciplinary approaches to politics. Alongside the expectable problems – relationship difficulties, early traumas, feelings of emptiness – we see the ecological and other crises presented as sources of symptoms and of unhappiness in individuals. From a psychological point of view, the world is making people unwell and it follows that, for people to feel better, the world's situation needs to change. Perhaps this is too passive: for people to feel better, maybe they have to recognize that the human psyche is a political psyche and do something about the state the world is in.

I sent a questionnaire to 2,000 analysts and therapists worldwide in which I asked them what political issues their clients mentioned in therapy, how they reacted, and what their own political views were (see Samuels, 1993, pp. 209–66). Aside from the revelation that the therapy profession is far more politically sensitive than one would think and that politics is a welcome theme in quite a few clinical offices, it was clear that clients are bringing economic, environmental and gender political issues to their therapy sessions much more than they used to. I think this development in the therapy world justifies my wider claim that, in our age, we are witnessing the emergence of a new kind of politics.

One role for psychology and the psychotherapies would be to mount a challenge to accepted ideas of what constitutes 'human nature'. At the moment, when idealistic or even utopian political thinking gets a bit threatening to the old order and to established ways of doing things, someone usually says, 'But what you're proposing goes against human nature!' What the speaker means is that human nature is violent, greedy, involves hostility to other people, and inevitably leads to a pecking order and social hierarchy. If such speakers are psychotherapists, then it is usually (and understandably) assumed that they are experts in human nature.

However, I am not sure that there really are objective experts in human nature. Most statements about human nature reflect the social circumstances, ideological prejudices and even the personality of the writer, not to mention his or her purpose in writing. Here the tag 'his or her' is very relevant because males and females are usually portrayed differently by writers on human nature. What they say varies over time. For example, according to novels and letters of the period, men in Europe stopped crying at the end of the eighteenth century. Up to then, it was perfectly manly to cry. Similarly, some ancient Greek philosophers said that women do not have souls.

In spite of these arguments, many people continue to assert conservatively that human nature is one thing that does not change over time. However, the fact that people may always have had similar emotional and physical experiences does not mean that they experienced these experiences in the same way. For the means they have to tell us about it are totally embedded in the worlds in which they lived.

One follow-on from this is that if it is possible to speak in terms of human nature changing it is very difficult to say that something is politically impossible because of human nature. What psychotherapists can contribute is an explanation of why more positive aspects of human nature have such a struggle to emerge. Psychotherapists can join academic critics in pointing out that the depressing definitions of human nature that are around are not neutral – someone benefits from them: big business, conventional politicians, reactionary males, anyone with a stake in the system has an interest in preserving the system's conception of human nature. For example, ask yourself who benefits when we are told that environmentalism and all kinds of new ideas for economic policy are unrealistic or too idealistic because of human nature being so greedy and selfish.

Some might ask if all of this is a New Age point of view. Well, Oscar Wilde wasn't exactly New Age and he said that, 'The only thing we know about human nature is that it changes. Change is the one quality we can predict of it ... The systems that fail are those that rely on the permanency of human nature, and not on its growth and development' (Wilde, 1978, p. 1,010).

It seems to me that self-exploration, self-development, self-expression – the whole interior thing that therapy does reasonably well – and political activity, conceived of rather broadly, are part of the same process. This realization is part of the big changes in politics that I have mentioned. Clinton and the Republicans won the elections in 1992 and 1994 respectively by intuiting that for many millions of people in the United States, politics and political choices, as expressed in the crudity of voting, had become matters of self-exploration and then self-expression. When we look at our lives from the point of view of political ideas and commitments, what we see is an unfolding of the personality in political terms.

I am concerned to address the fantasy that many engaged on an attempted transformation of politics still have that politics is only a dirty business, that getting involved in politics somehow sullies one, leading inevitably to a loss of self-respect. I challenge the divide that has arisen between what we ordinarily conceive of as creativity, self-respect and a productive inner life on the one hand and the political life on the other. Nowhere is this divide more clearly seen than in relation to economics.

Why economics?

Why is a focus on economics so important to any transformation of politics today? A friend said, 'Nobody will dispute that economics is important, but they'll all have different reasons why.'

The first reason – and I am sure for me it is the most compelling one, naïve as it might be to admit it – is an ethical reason. Because of economic thinking and economic systems people are suffering and dying. It does not seem right, and I think that anyone with a political conscience should commit himself or herself to evaluating what is going on in the economic sphere.

Secondly, economics is extraordinarily influential on all of us and on the cultures in which we live. Paul Samuelson, Nobel Laureate and writer of the most widely used standard text on economics, said, 'Let those who will write the nation's laws, just so long as I can write its textbooks.' Those who have studied economics at school or university will have read Samuelson. In the 1930s John Maynard Keynes made the claim that, 'Practical men [his word, men] who believe themselves to be quite exempt from any intellectual influences, are usually the slaves of some defunct economist.' Economics exerts an extremely powerful influence on all of us. But a damaging mystification has arisen around economic matters and, in spite of the fantastic changes in economic behaviour, organization and thinking over the past 250 years, citizens are all too often supposed to believe in today's preferred economic theory as if it were written in stone.

The third reason for focusing on economics has to do with credibility. Here am I, a psychotherapist, someone who spends a good deal of time and earns most of his money doing clinical work, trying to say something about the wider world of politics. How am I going to avoid being taken as some kind of flake? When I give interviews I try to get the flake thing in first. Better I should say I'm a flake than the interviewer should say it. This is a problem that anybody crossing disciplinary boundaries has to face, and economics is a difficult topic anyway. We do not seem very competent at the things we did not formally learn to do. I freely confess that, when it comes to economics, I do not really hack it all that well if I allow the professional economists to set the agenda. Nevertheless, the reason why economics is important is that, no matter how flaky a psychotherapist seems to be, if she or he shows interest in economics, and has something to say about economics, then politicians will listen, at least initially. It is a viable way to enter the political place, more viable, in the first instance, than making statements about gender, or environmentalism, or conflict resolution. Economics gets one listened to and therefore there is a rhetorical strategy behind paying attention to economics. I focus on issues of economics and class because these are the hard-edged, down-to-earth, real-world themes of our times. If psychologically oriented writers like me do not address economic topics, they will deservedly fail a credibility test.

Retraining the psyche

In my workshops on the 'economic psyche', I asked participants to imagine what would happen if they were told that the job they do was about to be made totally unnecessary for some reason. What other jobs could they do? What new skills would they need? How long do they think it will take to become competent in the new area of work?

Probably most of us know someone whose employment is threatened by technological innovation, international competition or cultural shifts. Even psychotherapists are susceptible to such pressures! This is why the exercise I have just outlined produces such extraordinarily powerful emotional responses with people from many different backgrounds breaking down in tears over the issues thrown up. Many political commentators have noted that in most Western countries the well-known employment problems of male manual workers whose rustbelt industries are moribund are just one aspect of a global transformation in labour economics. In countries like Britain, Germany and the United States, the fear of vocational extinction has spread deep into the middle classes. And, as we know, when social stresses hit the middle classes, the world is going to hear about it! For these are not people in the traditionally disempowered groupings. Nor are they rednecks or dinosaurs. They are people very much like those that I imagine are reading this piece.

The fact that no one can assume they have a job for life means that in the course of a working life each of us is going to have many jobs. This means that our employability will be directly connected to our adaptability and flexibility. We will have to convince employers and maybe tell ourselves that we can learn, meaning that we can learn on the job. These qualities of adaptability and flexibility are, of course, psychological characteristics and hence subject to all the usual psychological vicissitudes that we know about. But they are not yet much discussed by depth psychologists.

As part of my activities connecting politics and depth psychology, I was invited to attend a conference organized in London in 1994 by a Labour Party think tank on training and retraining for work. The conference was addressed by US Labor Secretary Robert Reich and Labour's Shadow Chancellor of the Exchequer Gordon Brown. They told us that we are entering the age of education-driven economics. Training and retraining are the keys to a successful modern economy.

Bearing in mind my experiences in the workshops, I was struck by the casual manner in which the huge collective psychological changes necessary for this kind of thinking to be effective were addressed. Actually, the emotional impact of perpetual retraining for successive, different jobs in the course of a lifespan was not truly addressed at all. But if these proposals, paralleled in many Western countries and having the support of many opinion-formers and policy-makers, are not to be defeated by massive, passive – or active – resistance, then the collective psychological dimension should not be left out.

What Reich and Brown referred to as the 'permanent educational revolution' in the world of work is going to affect women and men differently. This is not because women and men have inherently different psychological make-ups which express themselves totally differently in the world of work. Rather, it is the rigidly inscribed arrangements by which the genders are organized that make it important to distinguish between the likely reactions of women and men to the new economic regime that is being proposed and (probably) is going to happen. What follows is very much informed by what I learned at the 'economic psyche' events.

Many women will probably feel that they are already displaying the kind of economic flexibility these politicians are advocating. A woman's life often involves her in entering and leaving the world of work as she responds to society's demands for her to fulfil her so-called female role as carer of children. Yet most countries do not really reward flexibility and many do not even facilitate it. Being flexible at work so often means being low-paid at work – it's a specific example of the worldwide problem of the feminization of poverty in which women (and hence children) bear the brunt of recession and economic dislocation.

Women have spoken and written eloquently of the balancing

acts they have to perform so as to keep all their various social roles in psychological harmony. Of course, the result is never very harmonious and many women know that the approved goal of achieving an integration of all the roles and a settled, single identity is just part of what psychoanalyst Joan Rivière called the 'female masquerade'. A con trick, in other words, that many women have to use to avoid the psychological tensions between social oneness and social manyness.

This means that it is not at all certain that women will rush to embrace the new labour economics of Messrs. Reich and Brown. At the conference, there was altogether too much of a top-down rather than a bottom-up tone. These new strategies for re-employment do not show much respect for women's indigenous knowledge. How do women remake themselves time and time again? Are the (male) politicians going to try and find out?

At the workshops, one thing that we have experimented with is what it feels like to start to train oneself to do a new job well before the old job is played out – a kind of constructively schizoid attitude to work. Women's balancing acts have been a useful source of mentoring here. Another thing that has emerged is that training will be more effective if it is placed within a generally enriching framework and not confined to precise techniques learned and applied at the workplace. What the politicians consider to be 'education' may be psychologically demeaning. There's no reason in principle why work should not be a form of self-expression but we have to make a start by treating it as such. If education becomes too work-oriented, its capacity to release people's potential will be stunted.

For men, the problems with the new labour economics are even more psychologically intense and more likely to lead to a political impasse. I think it is possible for men to go beyond what has been called 'victim envy' to see what can be done about the changes in the workplace that are affecting them psychologically. I mentioned earlier the commonplace that there are special problems for unskilled men in localities where traditional industries have vanished. Far from having a job for life, they face life with nary a job in sight. Their grasp on authority, power and dignity is removed and many will bear emotional scars. If you cannot rely on what you know today being true and useful tomorrow, then your whole world-view is undermined.

In many respects, the Reich–Brown recipe fits perfectly into a cultural moment in the West when male supremacy in the political, social and economic spheres is being challenged from a number of quarters. One could scarcely say that the challenge has been very successful as yet, and the backlash certainly *was* effective, but the way in which social and cultural issues around masculinity (violence, sexual abuse, job insecurity, the backlash against feminism) have forced their way on to the political agenda in the past five years is striking. What this suggests to me – and I get this from all the psychological texts on 'men' as well – is that male certitudes are crumbling.

When men have to admit that there is no door-opening knowledge to which they have special access, then they are facing a full-frontal psychological onslaught on their dominant position in culture. How will men react to what they experience as an economic plague?

Many men are already feeling a sense of betrayal and are looking for scapegoats. But the sense of betrayal is more profound than can be assuaged by blaming feminists or rioting in the inner city. What is being betrayed is the false promise of masculinity itself – what I call 'the male deal'.

In the male deal, the little boy, at around four or five years old, strikes a bargain with the social world in which he lives. If he will turn away from soft things, feminine things, maternal things, from the world of play wherein failure doesn't matter, then the world will reward him by giving him all the goodies in its possession – all the women he can eat. In return for the gift of power, he promises to be a good provider and to keep unruly and subversive women and children in their places.

One question I want to pose is whether or not we can reframe the busting of the male deal as an opportunity to rethink a number of things: the deal itself and its damaging as well as pleasurable effects on men; the nature of male authority and its roots in Western attitudes to work (though there are signs this may be changing); the possibility of women and men facing the difficult economic times ahead as partners as well as adversaries.

I believe there is something at stake here in terms of the evolution of Western consciousness. We are witnessing a redefining by politicians who have not thought it through of what we understand by knowledge and skill. They are seeking to retrain the psyche. In the long term, the unmanning of work may bring all manner of benefits to the community – which is not to deny the short-term emotional hell many men will go through. For women, while the hell may be the hell they know already, it will be particularly galling to see what gains there have been swept away, not by simplistic men's movement gurus, but by the inexorable collective power of man-centred economic forces. So women, too, might want to explore what work could come to mean in the next century.

For women and men, gender issues will be at the heart of key economic debates in the years ahead. And that means that psychology will be in there, too. Gender itself is a hybrid, straddling disciplines that try to define it. On the one hand, gender is an absolutely private story we tell to ourselves about who we are and what we desire. On the other hand, gender is caught up in a web of socio-economic realities in the public world. The personal is not only political – it is also economic.

The new debate

If the personal is economic, then many aspects of economics will respond well to a psychological approach. For example, I believe that, from the standpoint of both psychology and politics, the old debate between the free marketeers and those who believed in a government-planned economy is played out. Despite electoral slogans, particularly in the United States, nobody in positions of influence is emotionally invested in either extreme position any more. It is important to stress this because so much progressive political energy is still being wasted in rectitudinous diatribes against the free market. But numerous books have now been written to show that what we thought was a free market in the neo-liberal heyday of the 1980s was simply not one. The Gingrich revolution will not produce a free market either. Nor will people ever enjoy a free market in the Eastern European countries or the Third World. This debate about the free market, in which I used to like to play an active part, has simply fizzled out. Even on the right, the issue is put in terms of restricting 'big' government or 'cutting' entitlements – the idealization of no government at all and virtually no taxes could not hold.

Nevertheless, I feel that we still need to go deeply into an exploration of the psychology of the market economy because, whether it exists or not, the market economy has become a worldwide numinous image. By numinous, I mean that the market economy as an image, as an idea, as a catchphrase, has captivated people whether they wanted to be captivated or not. When something numinous enters the picture, things polarize. The polarization in relation to the market economy was plain for everyone to see. On the one hand, we had those who believed that the market economy is the only economic system that works and is the guarantor of freedom, liberty and democracy. On the other hand, we had those who saw the market and its ruthlessness as lying behind the despoliation of the planet, resource wars, exploitation of women and children, and the gradual ruining of the future for our descendants.

When confronted with two such extreme verdicts on the same complicated socio-economic phenomenon – the market economy – what were we to do? We had to choose, or felt we had to choose. This psychologically exciting compulsion to choose has blinded us to the more sober fact that the debate about the market is politically moribund. Intellectually, most of us probably knew already that we had contradictory feelings about the free market. We knew that, on the one hand, it did often seem to generate resources, to be productive in the broadest sense. On the other hand – and we looked at Reagan's America or Thatcher's Britain when we said this – it did seem also inevitably to lead to social destruction, to waste of resources, to unfairness and to a kind of moral anarchy.

What has taken the life and energy away from the debates about market or government-planned economies has been the emergence of a new set of economic ideas and policies different from both the free market and a planned economy. I want to discuss some of these new economic ideas, using the knowledge and concepts of psychology and the psychotherapies to evaluate their viability, realism, creativity and contribution to achieving social justice.

Let us consider some of the alternative economic ideas that are around. Some of these will be familiar, others may not be. The dominant alternative economic idea around concerns sustainable development or sustainable growth. Living on a bounded planet, we do not use resources we cannot replace. We only use resources that we can replace within a realistic time frame. The problem with the idea of sustainable development is that, if we work it out statistically, what we have to conclude is that the whole of the world should function economically at approximately the level Portugal was at in 1960. Some would say that the way of life in Portugal in 1960 was not so terrible. Others are plain horrified at such authoritarian idealism. But, as a metaphor to guide us into the complexities of sustainable development, Portugal in 1960 will serve to illustrate how different sustainability is from the expansionist values of both a government-planned economy and a market economy.

Another alternative economic idea has to do with a redistribution of wealth between the countries of North and South, trying to reverse the present situation wherein, because of debt and interest repayments, there is actually a capital flow from the poorer countries to the richer countries, from the underdeveloped to the overdeveloped. This was certainly not the intention of international-aid policies over the past thirty-five or forty years, but it has become the outcome of those policies. Hence, there is a stress in alternative economic thinking on making it plain that our relative affluence is achieved at the expense of their relative poverty, and that rich and poor worldwide are psychologically linked by such financial and economic processes. Such an idea is anathema to free-marketeers.

A third piece of alternative economic thinking has to do with its pronounced commitment to environmentalist principles. One idea in particular interests me and this is the notion that there are what might be called global commons. These include the atmosphere, the oceans and those parts of the planet which have not yet been thoroughly settled such as the Arctic and Antarctic Circles. The idea of global commons is extraordinarily radical because it transcends the notion of ownership. Albeit the most provocative and difficult to assimilate, it is one of a whole range of environmentalized economic ideas that alternative economic thinking is bringing to bear on problems of pollution or the greenhouse effect.

A fourth alternative economic idea is that special attention needs to be paid to women's situation in the present-day economies of the West because of the growth of the feminization of poverty. Women suffer disproportionately at times of recession and benefit relatively less in times of economic recovery. This is something that used to be thought happened only in the Third World but now it is absolutely clear that it happens in Western countries as well. In the last ten years women, and hence children, get poorer more rapidly than men.

Finally, in terms of power, the new economic thinking struggles to get a better balance, a more workable balance, between the global, national, local and individual levels of power.

What all this adds up to is an entire value shift – a profound, complex, unbearable, perhaps doomed-to-fail psychological shift in our philosophies of life, and that has implications for the way we live. It means a quality-of-life retrenchment. It means a disavowal of the idea of economic progress.

Are the alternative economic ideas psychologically and politically realistic and feasible? I answer: yes and no. They are not realistic and feasible in the sense that they could be adopted immediately, easily or practically. It is also very difficult to see at first glance how human greed, competitiveness and love of the good life can in any way be disciplined or turned back. At the same time, quite a lot of this thinking and the values that inform it are already penetrating surprising places. Business corporations are starting to think about decentralization. The civil services of the West are starting to consider taxing polluters and alternative economics is getting into governmental discourse following the Earth Summit in Rio in 1992. At the moment, this influence is strictly at the level of reports, documents, think tanks, committees and the like. But, who knows? It may be something that is going to find a wider acceptance. One final mark of the realism of alternative economics is that a best-selling economic book in Britain and America in 1993 was called *Alternative Economic Indicators*. Even within the economics profession, bastion of resistance to ideas about sustainable development, there is a recognition that we could perhaps look for alternative ways of measuring the good life.

As I suggested, at the deepest levels these ideas have rendered the old pro- or anti-market debate redundant, because a new and equally fascinating debate has begun to emerge. The psychological intricacies of the debate can be equally clearly discerned in the United States and in Britain. This new debate is between those whom I term the *modified marketeers* and another group that I call the *alternative economists* and it picks up on that tension between feasibility and idealism that has caused so much trouble for the Green parties and for environmental politics generally. Often an individual – economist or plain citizen – will experience this psychological tension within him or herself.

The modified marketeers aim at a 'social market', meaning an economic system that provides a degree of governmental regulation of business and finance plus a safety net for those who do not make it. They are interested in increasing productivity via government encouragement of investment in new technology and equipment and extensive retraining programmes, though they have some green sensibilities about pollution and so forth.

The modified marketeers believe that, in general terms, the system can be made to work better, meaning in a way that combines efficiency and social justice. We see modified marketeers in the Labour Party, the Clinton administration and American politics generally, the Western European social democratic parties, ruling circles in Eastern Europe and sometimes even in the vibrant economies of the Pacific rim. The modified marketeers are strong on realism and relatively weak on value change.

The alternative economists, on the other hand, following Schumacher ('small is beautiful'), are weaker on realism and strong on value change, having many interesting and challenging things to say about the way we live in the West today.

The alternative economists are devoted to changing our values and the way these inform thinking about economics. They are not interested in productivity but prefer, following a wide range of ecologistic or environmentalist philosophies, to explore dismantling the industrial infrastructures in pursuit of sustainable development and a more just economic and trade balance between the countries of North and South. The alternative economists want to decentralize economic activity; they try to respect local knowledge and ways of doing things (change seen as coming from below) and are challenging conventional wisdoms by, for example, experimenting with local currency schemes in which ordinary money would not be used. The alternative economists are also interested in areas such as retraining but for quite different reasons to those given by the modified marketeers: not for productivity, but for an enhancement of the quality of life, seeing work as a form of self-expression and self-creation. Similarly, the environmentalism of the alternative economists is far more radical than the greening of production methods sought by the modified marketeers.

Now it is not necessary to agree totally with my depiction of this debate (though many politicians and economists in America and Britain have said spontaneously that it resonates for them and that they do feel torn in just this way). The point is that this is a *debate between progressives*, between individuals and groups whose hearts are *all* in the right place! Those who advocate feasibility, programmes for economic regeneration and recovery and so forth, are not somehow less moral or less full of integrity than those who call for a complete shift in world view and the dismantling of capitalism altogether. A good deal of attention has been paid by the modified marketeers to rendering the market more compassionate, to tenderizing the market, creating capitalism with a human face. But what if we were to switch the emphasis to toughening the alternative economists, by subjecting these resacralizers to co-existence with the more dispassionate modified marketeers? My claim is that there's everything to play for provided the men and women of vision access their reserves of realism and the men and women of realism access their reserves of vision.

Psychological economics

Feasibility and idealism – can they ever be brought together in human affairs generally, and in the economic sphere in particular? This is, fundamentally, a psychological question. I have been trying to see how we might introduce psychology to economics via the psychoanalytic concept of ambivalence – meaning the capacity to have contradictory feelings (usually love and hate) towards the same person or phenomenon at the same time – in this case wealth and wealth creation. When Eugen Bleuler coined the term in 1910 he meant to indicate that ambivalence was a pathology but, as time passed, theorists began to see that there are forms of ambivalence that are also emotional milestones, achievements of increasing psychological maturity (Jung, 1916; Klein, 1935). To be ambivalent in relation to the economics debate between modified marketeers and alternative economics would not mean trying to combine or synthesize the best features of two approaches. If that is supposed to be the goal then it will not be satisfactorily achieved because something central to each would be lost. But what if each economic philosophy were to be allowed to develop in its own particular way? What might happen then?

We would begin to state openly that, while we do not want *rich capitalists* with all the destructiveness and inequality they bring, we do want *wealth-creating entrepreneurs* with all the social benefits that their productivity undeniably brings. We want the entrepreneurs because they do create the wealth. We do not want them to become very rich capitalists because that leads to the kind of shitty, unfair, death-dealing, planet-despoiling system we do not like. How could we get to a situation in which there were entrepreneurs who did not become capitalists? Could we rescue the idea of the market from capitalism in some way?

We could limit the permitted turnover of private companies headed by entrepreneurs. We could say – and this is ambivalence in the economic sphere in action – we could say: 'OK, up to three-quarters of a million you can have a private company. After that, a degree of public or social ownership needs to be introduced.' The community must have a say after a certain wealth-point has been reached. Or we could make it illegal for an entrepreneur to borrow money privately from banks after his personal wealth and that of his company had reached a certain point. We would decide, by the usual processes of political debate, what that point would be. The idea is to struggle to get to terms with our contradictory feelings about wealth and not polarize the feelings. We need to go beyond *either* wanting to stop budding entrepreneurs in their tracks *or* wanting them to be able to go on and become Bill Gates or Rupert Murdoch. My psychological approach to economic policy involves some practical limitations being placed on the growth of private companies and on the ways in which they are permitted to finance themselves. It would be a radical form of the 'stakeholding' proposed as a central economic idea by the Labour Party in Britain at the end of 1995 (and see below for further discussion of stakeholding).

But not everyone is going to be an entrepreneur. Is it impossible to create a psychological atmosphere in which we teach and encourage entrepreneurial skills but we do not stigmatize or criticize entrepreneurial failures? 'Try to get rich, but if you don't make it, don't feel bad about it. Failure is inevitable.' At the moment the message is that business failure is a very serious business, almost a moral flaw.

In terms of the institutions required, we would need a plurality of economic institutions, ranging from private companies to large state corporations, with co-operatives (like the Mondragon co-operatives in the Basque country) somewhere in the middle. It would mean not committing ourselves to only one style of economic organization, a pluralistic position which is psychologically difficult to hold to. But I believe that psychology, in the way I am positioning it, fosters the adoption of a plurality of differing economic organizational styles. I think that there would be a special role for pension funds or similar institutions because these are in a sense already socialized or collective institutions. Their role would be enhanced in the kind of economic proposals that I am exploring.

If we encouraged success but did not punish failure, then we have a psychological background that would make proper, decent, minimum-wage legislation an inevitability — not something to argue about any more. One reason why so many Western countries do not have effective minimum-wage legislation may be because they are so hooked up on this success–failure divide. Exhorting success but not penalizing failure also leads to the consideration of ideas like social dividends or credits, which would replace social security and welfare systems.

Ultimately, if we did manage to allow ambivalence about wealth to come into being, we might end up with a substantial sector of the economy that was simply outside the business world altogether, that was not money-fuelled, did not use money in the ordinary way, in which exchange of services, perhaps by voucher systems or local currency systems might come into being. The beginnings of such a development can be observed in several countries.

There are some wider things to consider here such as the relatively new idea of 'social audit'. An audit is a way of measuring the financial situation of a company. But a social audit measures things which have usually been regarded an non-measurable in financial terms. In a sense, a social audit is a psychological project. In a social audit, we try to measure the *ethical* profit-and-loss situation of an organization by looking at what it is doing in relation to what it seeks to do, and above all by looking at what it is doing in relation to what its 'stakeholders', who are not only the shareholders but also the employees and customers, want to do with their company. Becoming psychological about economics means that certain inhibitions on thought get removed, and we can start to think in terms of measuring the unmeasurable, of carrying out an 'emotional audit' of economic and business activity.

I am aware that some of these ideas have been floated before, especially by those on the left. What is perhaps novel in this psychologized version is that there is a conscious attempt being made to enjoy two sides of an argument, to get the benefit of both perspectives rather than resolving them into a spurious synthesis which will usually end up by favouring the modified marketeers, alloys being easier to work than gold. *The result looks contradictory because it is supposed to be contradictory*, taking energy off the interplay and tension of competing viewpoints (cf. Samuels, 1993, pp. 88–94). As the right-wing economist Milton Friedman once said: 'The more significant the theory, the more unrealistic the assumptions.'

I suggest that we consider how to extend the vocabulary of economics. If we use the metaphor of an iceberg where a seventh is above the surface and six-sevenths below the surface, then we can argue that most economic analysis takes place only in the top part. There are endless arguments about how much it would cost to do this or that, or what the alternative benefits in terms of goods or services might be.

But we could begin to think beyond 'exchange value' (cost or price) to consider 'emotional value', 'aesthetic value' and 'sustainable value'. For example, developers or government departments favour road-building at the expense of the environment or mammoth supermarkets in a conservation area. Perhaps a case can be made for doing it in terms of exchange value. We could argue that the emotional value of the environment or conservation may be far greater than that of the road or supermarket. The development would also sacrifice aesthetic value. And if trees and natural habitats are destroyed, then long-term sustainability is reduced.

There are emotional costs for all of us living in a system characterized by extremes of inequality in the distribution of wealth. Connections between physical health and wealth have been extensively mapped, including the impact of unemployment, alienation in the workplace and changing patterns of employment. Less often discussed are the psychological consequences of deficiencies in economic and social justice on those who apparently are reasonably well situated. To live in an unfair economic system has a poor effect on all of us, leading to widespread anxiety about economic well-being.

What do you really feel about economics?

A particular psychological aspect of economics that I have been exploring in workshops concerns what people feel about money and about equality and inequality of wealth. If we really wanted to, we surely could do away with economic injustice. Hence, it becomes crucial to discover why it is that we do not want to do away with economic injustice, why we just love inequality. In these workshops two themes often emerge. First, how difficult it is in terms of self-respect for well-meaning persons to admit openly how much they love inequality of wealth. This discovery, and the creation of a safe space in which to confess to materialism, is in itself of psychological interest. But it is the second theme that was totally unexpected. Alongside the love of money, the flaunting fantasies and the sadistic play – and often in the very same people – there is an equally powerful and active turning away from all that is involved in an espousal of inequality of wealth. You have to wade through fantasies of ostentation and exploitation of others to reach the equally secret disgust-driven commitment to a more fair economic system. But it is there, masked in part by our rules about having a consistent view in areas of serious public concern such as economics. For example, although it is easy to poke fun at people who are responsible for resource-greedy and polluting factories seeking rural solace in a simpler life at weekends, the fact that so many middle-class people turn to the countryside and the great outdoors for spiritual refreshment perhaps shows that there is some energy available for the reduction of inequalities of wealth (cf. Parker, 1995, for an account of the creative impact of maternal ambivalence on mothering; the argument is analogous to that proposed here).

The meanings that any individual attributes to money are learned to a great extent in the family. Cash may be clung to or thrown away because of its hoped-for potential to make up for a sense of loss or to provide emotional warmth; to give an individual personal worth, express longings that cannot be articulated in any other way or establish contact with others. It is these emotional elements that explain the intensity of the feelings people experience in relation to money. Attitudes to money are also shaped by experiences of the wider world and it is the interaction between social experience and personal history that explains individual responses to such developments as increasing insecurity in employment or the crumbling of the welfare state.

The key thing about bringing psychology to economics is that we are enabled to see something very tangible in the economic world, something material, as suffused with emotion and fantasy.

Owning up to our complex feeling about wealth means owning our own criminality as well as our generosity. As the Moscow Mafia presently demonstrates, at the heart of market economics lies a form of economic criminality. Proudhon's 'property is theft' is one instance of a similar thought from the past. But our economic criminality also links us to something that we probably value rather highly: our ingenuity and improvisation, the work of the trickster in economics, shown in the burgeoning informal 'parallel economies' of the world (such as the cocaine trade) without which people would, quite simply, die of starvation. In Lima, one in two of the population is sustained by the informal parallel economy. Let's think about this: on the one hand, criminality, unfairness, cheating, lying, stealing, death. On the other hand, ingenuity, energy, imagination, inspiration, improvisation, productivity, life. Psychological economics is not consistent; it requires us to relate to all these contradictory things in ourselves at the same time. We cannot just dispense with the problems of the psychology of theft because we want to enjoy the fruits of the psychology of economic ingenuity.

In the Appendix, I list of some of the questions explored in the workshops. While I would not claim that such workshops accurately represent 'real life', the participants come from a very wide range of occupational and economic backgrounds and certainly do their best to convey, in psychological terms, what their daily economic existence is like. It is an example of extending the usual remit of 'emotional literacy' from private, emotional, relationship concerns into the public sphere.

Psychotherapy, psychoanalysis and economics

Economic motivation is not something separate that can be analysed in isolation. To bring psychology and the psychotherapies to economics merely as an explanation for economic behaviour runs the risk of reductionism that I mentioned earlier and I think this has marred many previous attempts to link the two. Rather, I prefer to use them to bring out the symbolic and psychological underpinning of the economic institutions, processes and ideas that we have come to take as concrete aspects of a rational world. Here, I am with Freud and his seminal observation that instinctual needs can never be truly satisfied on the bodily level alone. When they seem to be, this will have involved psychological as well as biological processes.

A psychological economics appreciates from the outset that there will always be degrees of wastefulness and uncontrollability in economic systems. Once human desire gets into any social system, its functioning will be unpredictable. It is to the eroticized operations of desire (including physical sexuality and struggles over sexual orientation) rather than to something like chaos theory that I look in order to get to grips with the shock that there are no final solutions to social questions.

The social issues with which our societies are faced are as incorrigible, as unresponsive to treatment, as the psychological issues that individuals face. Just as we now know there is no unified ego that stands in for the whole personality, there is also no one unified economic citizen with a coherent agenda, and no unified version of society either. This is what makes control of the social impossible. In today's consumption-oriented economies, it is probably to mass or collective psychology that we must look to get a handle on the irrationality of the economic forces that we are subject to. But there are no universal social forms to fall back on, no essentialist economic archetypes that would sort all this out for us. We have to start with as open a mind as possible, paying free-floating, evenly hovering attention to economic matters.

In spite of the difficulties of the task that faces us, I do wonder if the pessimistic tone of much contemporary psychoanalytic social criticism, especially in the Lacanian tradition, does not reflect a secret idealization of the impossibility of modifying the social dilemmas which we face. This would amount to a surrender to the death drive. A psychoanalytic critic whose stress is on the permanent state of social rupture that exists within a hegemonically structured society, and whose understanding is that human subjectivity is contingent on a fundamental sense of lack, isn't going to be disappointed when constructive political intentions go awry or economic processes spiral out of control. Their theory predicts that this is bound to happen and they say that to expect a positive outcome is infantile and grandiose.

I want to argue that such discourses of lack and rupture, and those founded on the claim that there is an infantile component in the making of economic policy, grossly restrict our conception of what subjectivity consists of, especially subjectivity as lived in the social and political realms. It is as if, in the rush to be worldly wise and theoretically correct, some psychoanalytic political theorists from diverse schools have lost sight of vital areas of human experience that go beyond linguistic and infantile phenomena. Human beings are both made by *and* make the culture in which they live. The psyche is both conservative and creative. The value of keeping a psychoanalytic health warning in the picture is for its reminder that, painful though it is to accept, we might fail to make the changes we aspire to in a time frame that feels emotionally acceptable. Psychoanalysis provides us (and itself, perhaps) with a cold douche of realism.

Appendix

QUESTIONS EXPLORED AT WORKSHOPS ON 'THE ECONOMIC PSYCHE':

1   What are the three most pressing economic problems facing the US (or UK)?
2   What are your solutions?
3   What are the three most pressing economic problems facing the world?
4   What are your solutions?
5   Do you find economics mystifying?
6   What aspects of economics would you like to know more about?

7 In what format would you like to learn more? (e.g. distance learning, seminars, etc.)

8 How much more in taxation would you be prepared to pay if you approved of what the money would do?

9 What things would you prefer not to pay taxes for?

10 What are your feelings and attitudes towards the very wealthy?

11 Do you feel that economic issues have got out of the control of our government?

12 What can be done about unemployment?

13 Do you agree that we should not consume more resources than we can replace?

14 If this means giving something up, what could you give up?

15 What are your memories of money issues in your childhood?

16 How did your family handle money?

17 Was money talked about at home?

18 Have you 'done better' than your parent(s)?

19 How do you feel about the answer to the last question?

20 How do you handle money issues in your personal relationships now?

21 Have you ever had fantasies about having lots of money?

22 What are they?

23 Do you feel guilty about economic inequalities in the world – e.g. between First and Third World countries?

24 Do you think we in the West should draw back economically speaking?

25 Would you say that money and economic matters have injured the values you would like to stick to?

Acknowledgements

I am grateful for the helpful comments and criticisms on earlier drafts of this chapter from Michael Vannoy Adams, John Beebe, Rosie Parker, Fred Plaut, Sonu Shamdasani, John Southgate and David Tresane.

References

Hillman, J. & Venture, M. (1992), *We've had a Hundred Years of Psychotherapy and the World's Getting Worse*, New York: HarperCollins

Jung, C. G. (1916), 'The Transcendent Function', in *Collected Works*, Vol. 8., London: Routledge & Kegan Paul; Princeton, NJ: Princeton University Press

Klein, M. (1935), 'A Contribution to the Psychogenesis of Manic-Depressive States', in *Love, Guilt and Reparation and Other Works 1921–1945*, Virago, 1988

Parker, R. (1995), *Torn in Two: The Experience of Maternal Ambivalence*, Virago

Samuels, A. (1993), *The Political Psyche*, Routledge

Wilde, O. (1978), 'The Soul of Man under Socialism', in *Complete Works of Oscar Wilde*, Book Club Associates

Commentary
ECONOMIC GOODS

Andrew warns us at one point in his chapter that some people may think he is a bit of a flake – a psychotherapist talking about politics and economics – so he gets in first with this charge. But you can see the risk he runs, and that he knows it. In trying to combine impassioned commitment with intellectual argument, he may go too far for some. He is brimming with big concepts and ideas about the transformation of politics and about the new economic debate. It is compelling, inspiring reading, but has he been just too optimistic? Does he make it sound too easy? Does he link satisfactorily with our own everyday experience?

Let's take the idea of political energy. Andrew defines it as 'the capacity to bring imagination, creativity and effort to bear on seemingly intractable problems, to try to solve them in ways that reflect concern for social justice'. He suggests that all of us are born with and/or develop a certain amount of this energy. This is politics of a particular slant, concerned with equality and fairness. Presumably there are those with political energy of a different kind who seek to control and manipulate others into serving their own ends and preserving the *status quo*. Would Andrew see this as the negation of, or a corruption of, political energy, or as the inevitable negative aspect of such energy?

Is it possible to think of supportive evidence for Andrew's suggestion of different levels of political energy? Amnesty International comes to mind. A girl in her mid-teens recently told one of the editors that her mother had forbidden her to join it, as somehow not a nice or proper thing to get mixed up with. This feels like an example of a parent with little political energy and a daughter with potentially more of it.

Another of Andrew's concepts (drawn from his book *The Political Psyche*) is the 'psychological citizen' who is 'politically self-aware' and who knows that 'the personal, inner and private levels of life connect up with the political, outer and public levels'. This concept has been around in Jungian psychology for a few years. The American archetypal psychologist James Hillman also used the term in his lively exchange of letters with journalist Michael Ventura, published in 1992 under the title *We've had a Hundred Years of Psychotherapy and the World's Getting Worse*. Hillman wrote that 'every citizen is already concerned with the material nature of things ... but the special role of the psychological citizen is the awakening and refining of aesthetic sensitivity'. He identified one of the purposes of therapy as supporting the citizen's capacity to see 'what is invisibly going on ... within and behind events', and that this requires 'civil courage, just like the personal courage required in personal relationships. Civil courage ... means not only demanding social justice but also aesthetic justice and the will to make judgements of taste, to stand for beauty in the public arena and speak out about it' (pp. 125–6).

Hillman is talking about something a little different from Andrew, but what both are saying is that the old divide between thinking about what is going on inside us – the old stamping ground of counselling and psychotherapy – and what is going on all around us – the traditional haunt of politicians, planners and the 'practical' people – is breaking down. And that this brings with it tremendous possibilities, to which psychotherapy has a contribution to make.

One contribution Andrew suggests is to bring ambivalence out of disgrace. Psychotherapists have long recognized it as inevitable in all our deepest relationships, to be faced and accepted. But in public, and especially in political life, it is usually presented as a sign of weakness. Politicians are often at pains to claim that they have always held their current views, sensing that any hint of change or indecisiveness will render them vulnerable to charges of poor judgement or that most ringing of all taunts, being unfit for office. Do we really require our politicians to be paragons of sameness? In her chapter Dorothy Rowe argued the case for a scientific culture in which relativity and uncertainty are accepted. We tend to trust scientists and hold them in high regard even when, perhaps especially when, they express caution about the state of their knowledge. Could we extend this kind of regard to those in public life?

If we could learn to live with ambivalence in all spheres of life – our feelings towards our partners, our children and our parents, our workplace, politics, economics – might it take away much of the stress and tension that come from trying to convince ourselves to believe in only one side of our feelings. The fear seems to be that if we own up to our ambivalent feelings our capacity to make decisions, to take action, will be paralysed. Perhaps the lesson of psychotherapy is that the opposite is more true: that once we get our ambivalent feelings out in the open, we can relax more because the pressure of pretending is gone. A relaxed state of mind is much better for decision-making.

Andrew's optimism is nowhere more infectious than in his assertion that the old economic debate between free markets and planned economies has been replaced by a debate between supporters of alternative economics and a modified, socially responsible market, where 'both sides have their heart in the right place'. A 'no lose' situation, 'provided the men and women of vision access their reserves of realism and the men and women of realism access their reserves of vision'.

It sounds great. In practice it can only be painful and maybe even harder work than Andrew acknowledges. Anyone who has tried to combine altruism and profitability (or not making a loss), as a self-employed individual or in a small organization like a counselling service, will know only too well the struggle to balance vision and realism. Part of the problem seems to be that we feel offended, or at least taken aback, if our visionaries turn out to be realists, and amused or cynical if hard-headed realists start asserting their desire to do good. Example: the mother superior of an American convent succeeded in spanning the divide with a simple slogan, 'No margin – no Mission.' What a shocking thing for a nun to say! In accessing their alternative reserves the men and women Andrew is thinking of will need to overcome not only their own inclinations but the cultural stereotypes that exist around their activities.

Two other themes in Andrew's chapter connect closely with what other contributors have written. These are the impact of the changing nature of work and the question of how fixed human nature is. Like Eric Miller, Andrew notes that thinking about unemployment changed radically when it began to affect senior managers and professionals as much as the working classes, who have traditionally suffered. Andrew and Eric both comment on the apparent insensitivity of those in the driving seats, whether as captains of industry or politicians, to the psychological impact of the changes in the nature of work and of employment prospects. Eric describes the false rhetoric of worker empowerment and the anger and disbelief when 'disloyal managers' talk of building committed workforces. Andrew describes the casual manner in which the huge psychological changes necessary to enable us to live with a permanent educational revolution are treated. Few people, it seems, have fully grasped the nettle of how we are going to cope with these changes. Andrew suggests that one source of 'mentorship' may come from the experience women have always had of balancing the demands of child-care and work. But if this is taken to be an experience of 'fitting in, adapting down', then it will be of limited value to men who have to come to terms with giving up what he calls the 'male deal'.

Significantly, maybe ominously, Will Hutton (1995) writes that 'no state in the twentieth century has ever been able to recast its economy, political structures and society to the extent that Britain must do, without suffering defeat in war, economic collapse or revolution' (p. 318). Two world wars enabled women to be seen as valuable economic workers. Feminism, without a war or a revolution, has faced an uphill struggle in trying to change women's role in society. Does it take a war or revolution for human nature to change? One of the themes returned to by many of our contributors is that both the pace and the extent of change in our society are greater now than ever before. Perhaps this *is* the revolution, which is both frightening and rich in possibilities.

Andrew argues that human nature has never been as fixed as we suppose, and that those who dismiss ideas that human nature can change as over-optimistic usually have some self-interest up their sleeve. One such self-interest, he suggests, is the satisfaction experienced by some social critics of being proved right by each new piece of evidence of our moral, economic or social decline. But there is also the view, which Bob Hinshelwood advocates, that as we cannot help being passionate and evaluative we do better to recognize this rather than pretend to some objective neutrality.

The important question is what aspects need to change if we are to adapt, and are these aspects ones that are fixed or capable of changing? What needs to change according to Dorothy Rowe are our fear, greed, vanity and desire for power. Andrew argues that the psyche is both conservative and creative. When Margaret Thatcher uttered her famous remark that there was no such thing as society she epitomized the world of self-interest, and made less hospitable the climate for the other side of human nature that seeks to collaborate, create, have social justice, and could even stand taxation for the common good. It is as if that repressed side of our human nature is nudging around looking for a way back in. A revolution would break down the walls. But one of the lessons of history is that unless revolutions are truly from the bottom up we only replace one set of leaders with another and do little for the led. We may need to take the walls down a few bricks at a time.

Reference

Hutton, W. (1995), *The State We're In*, Jonathan Cape

Chapter 10
LIVING TOGETHER IN UNCERTAIN TIMES

David Kennard and Neil Small

We used the analogy in our introduction of editors acting as hosts. If we take this analogy just a little further we might describe our hosting a meal with the different writers providing separate dishes for you, the reader, to taste and enjoy. Some things would look and taste like dishes you had previously encountered. Others you might approach with a little trepidation; you hadn't come across this before. Maybe next time you are out you will try these things again. As hosts we have tried to help you negotiate the menu and choose a balanced meal. We gave a lot of thought to what was on offer and in what order you would be presented with the courses (but we expect you will have chosen your own order anyway). We have tried to talk between dishes in the way dinner-party hosts might keep things going, making connections and trying to keep a friendly ambience. We are now getting towards the end of dinner. We don't expect you to do the washing-up but, in this final part, we would like to offer you a tour of the kitchen.

We want to show something of the workings that underpin the ideas developed in the various chapters. This concluding chapter will therefore look at some of the assumptions underlying the book. It will concentrate in particular on macro-level social concerns. In so doing the chapter will disproportionately emphasize that part of the book which looks at social structures as opposed to those parts that consider the family and other intimate relationships. All our contributors have looked at the individual and society, and have chosen differing emphases. This chapter will not be different. Its concern will be to look at psychoanalysis and at social change and at the relationship between the two. In so doing the intention is to take some of the ideas our contributors draw on, develop them and put them in context. Richard Hoggart, writing in 1958 in the preface of his book *The Uses of Literacy*, says how he has 'written as clearly as my understanding of the subject allowed, and used technical terms and allusions only when they seemed likely, once known, to prove helpful and suggestive'. He goes on to say that the intelligent 'layman' is an elusive figure, and popularization a dangerous undertaking: 'But it seems to me that those of us who feel that writing for him is an urgent necessity must go on trying to reach him.'

Psychoanalysis and society

'[Freud is] no more a person now but a whole climate of opinion' (W. H. Auden, 1966)

From the early years of the twentieth century Freud's ideas, and those of other psychoanalysts, have been making their way into popular magazines and public discussion. At times of great stress, during the two world wars for example, there was both accelerated change within the discipline itself and a rise in the public prominence of psychoanalytic ideas and of their exponents. Two of the contributors to this volume have, elsewhere, charted some of this history. Bob Hinshelwood has written about the wide range of interest in Freud in the years from 1893 (the first point at which the work of Freud was noticed in Britain) until 1918, and Barry Richards has described various images of Freud in British psychology after the Second World War (Hinshelwood, 1995; Richards, 1989).

Freud appeared to be appropriated by various people acting within specific subject areas. As Bob puts it, 'Psychoanalysis was shrunk by each cultural site until Freud presented what the eyes of its members wished to see.' There was Freud the interpreter of symbols for the artistic community, Freud the exponent of a model of child development for the educationalists, Freud on sex for those interested in challenging the dominant assumptions about sexual desires and their social repression and so on.

If the popular presentation of Freud, and subsequently other psychoanalysts, has been around for nearly as long as the ideas themselves, there has been an even higher profile in recent years. Perhaps, as Philip Rieff argued in 1966, there has been a 'triumph of the therapeutic with the psychologizers fully established as the pacesetters of cultural change', or perhaps we are living within Guy Debord's 'society of the spectacle' where commentary and interpretation are perceived to be more meaningful than the event itself. Or perhaps it is both (Rieff, 1966; Debord, 1967).

Since 1982, when psychiatrist Anthony Clare started his long-running radio programme *In the Psychiatrist's Chair,* there has been a proliferation of media therapy. In 1990 psychiatrist Dr Raj Persaud was speculating in the *Guardian* about the mental state of Saddam Hussein. He went on to have a column in the *Daily Mail* and a slot on Breakfast TV. Dr Dennis Friedman, director of a private psychiatric clinic, comments on the royal family. There are columns in the tabloid Sundays; Dr Vernon Coleman in the *People* and clinical psychologist Dr Oliver James in the *Sunday Express.* Then, of course, there are the contributors to this book. Robin Skynner became widely known first via the book *Families and How to Survive Them* (which he wrote with John Cleese) and then through the press and radio. Susie Orbach, Valerie Sinason and Dorothy Rowe all regularly contribute to newspapers and magazines.

While it is clear that psychoanalytically informed writers in the popular media are continuing a tradition, there have been some subtle changes. First we now have, occupying a central role, people writing from within the discipline rather than commentors viewing from outside, or specialists from other areas seeking to assimilate specific aspects of the psychoanalytic approach. Second, although some of the people listed above would justify their public stance on the grounds of educating people about psychiatry or psychotherapy there is increasingly the presence of a group who are concerned to exercise some intervention in society. These writers look out from the theory and practice of psychoanalysis and explore its relevance to wider social structures and to the processes of social change.

Again this, in itself, is not new. In pre-Second World War Frankfurt members of the School of Social Research, which included Eric Fromm, often met with S. H. Foulkes, who subsequently founded the Institute of Group Analysis in London. Fromm explored the way psychoanalytic ideas could address social issues via work on what he saw as a 'fear of freedom' which expressed itself in abject submission to authority, including totalitarianism. Such approaches and critiques were not only intellectually challenging but were politically dangerous and psychoanalysts and sociologists had to flee their home countries as the Nazis consolidated their grip (Hearst, 1993; Fromm, 1943, 1949, 1970).

Like any movement, psychoanalysis has had periods of relative strength and times when even its friends were talking about crisis. Reductions in numbers of trainees and of patients and a problem in responding to the inroads of new kinds of therapy, offering quicker and cheaper 'cures', produced such responses in the late 1960s and 1970s. But there was also a regrouping and a reassertion that psychoanalysis offered a starting point that problematized both knowledge and culture, things were more complicated and doing things was harder than had previously been imagined. New factors were introduced into the agenda – science, technology, racism – and new approaches were addressed, most notably in responding to the challenges of feminism. Contributors to this book have played a part in this movement (Kitwood, 1988).

By the mid 1990s we can see the development of a series of organizational groupings seeking to bring people together to explore the issues of change and intervention, and also to lobby for an enhanced understanding of psychoanalytic issues at a social and political level. Indeed the genesis of this book is in just such a grouping. The development of a collective role for psychoanalysis and psychotherapy and their practitioners is evident in the activities of the Psychoanalysis and the Public Sphere Annual Conference, started in 1987. It is evident in the organization Psychotherapists and Counsellors for Social Responsibility, set up in 1995, and in Antidote, a group concerned with developing the emotional literacy of both individuals and organizations. Within British sociology there is a Sociology of the Emotions Study Group and a developing debate, for example in the journal *Sociology*, about cultural studies, emotions and psychoanalysis.

A social mission

This proliferation of organization might be a last-gasp attempt to generate a collective shout from the sidelines. But it might also be a recognition that the changes in the way we live our lives at the end of the millennium offer challenges, even opportunities, and not just grounds for feelings of hopelessness.

There is a need to restate what has always been the 'social mission of psychoanalysis'. Michael Rustin and Andrew Cooper put it like this in a plenary session of the Psychoanalysis and the Public Sphere Conference in 1995: 'The recognition of the ubiquity and normality of psychic pain, and of defences against it. The vulnerability of human lives, at their inevitable moments of stress and change, to encounters with the pressures of the "irrational", is what the psychoanalytic tradition compassionately insists on.' This compassion must be located within a strong sense of social dependency – a recognition that relationships and almost every human activity go hand in hand and that effectively to exercise authority of any kind requires the containment and toleration of anxiety and mental pain. A former president of the Psychoanalytic Society, Eric Brenman, argues that 'in understanding ourselves we will be more generously disposed to helping others'. It helps to 'replace the language of blame by the language of achievement' (*Guardian*, 12 June 1996).

Now, as we near the end of the century, we see presented in the various chapters contributed to this book a sense of accelerated and profound social change and a challenge to individuals, families and indeed societies that is perhaps greater than any challenge so far encountered. We also see a vigorous engagement with the challenges and opportunities these changing times present. It may be that, as Susie Orbach says in her chapter, psychoanalysis helps people read themselves retrospectively, but as she and our other writers demonstrate it also gives a framework to interrogate the present and hypothesize about the future.

It is not so much that there is still a fight to have the language of reflection and the importance of relationships accepted. Various contributors to this book have looked at different manifestations of the 'triumph of the therapeutic'. Barry Richards, for example, argues that popular culture (for him in the form of soap opera) provides evidence that this cultural shift has already occurred. Rather there is a recognition that we have to move on from merely having a script for how to respond to crisis, to an emotional engagement with other people.

Globalization, post-Fordism and consumerism

There are four features of the end of the millennium that create the environment of challenge and opportunity that psychoanalysis can engage with. All are changes in the wider world that can profoundly affect us as individuals. All are explored, overtly or tangentially, in our contributors' chapters. We will consider three here and then, in the next section, go on to postmodernism, the fourth. First is the phenomenon of globalization. This has many different dimensions including the breakdown of the sense of the meaningful boundary of the nation state which is seen by some as a profound problem in terms of identity. The protracted dispute in British political life about the European Union is no doubt in part about politicians' opportunism and in part based on a reasoned assessment of the political, economic and cultural impact of closer or weaker links. But, fundamentally, the debate addresses the felt sense of danger in being submerged in a greater whole. Such a fear has resonance within psychoanalysis as it seeks to reconcile dependency and autonomy in the development of the individual. Being submerged carries risks, so too does an isolation fuelled by insecurity. A narrow self-righteous nationalism has fuelled many of the atrocities of the century and also has parallel manifestation in the insecure individual.

Globalization is fuelled by information technology, by advances in transportation and by international finance and consumer capitalism. A particular feature of the last years of the twentieth century is that those in the industrialized world have easy access to whatever features of the world 'market forces' have decided are of interest. The Internet and the fax machine, allied to the TV and jet travel, have changed the way we view the spatial world. The internationalization of production, where products that could easily be made locally, and perhaps once were, are now imported from the far side of the earth, have changed patterns of production and consumption. This is an area explored in Eric Miller's chapter in this book. According to Christopher Lasch, in his 1995 book *The Revolt of the Elites and the Betrayal of Democracy*, there is now 'a transnational élite, global in its perspective, cosmopolitan in taste. It is not bound by tiresome traditional obligations such as a concern for less privileged fellow-citizens. It is a new ruling caste.' As such they are much more likely to invoke the global economy than the national interest when attempting to justify low wages or the reduction of workers' rights.

The 'Global Village' might be something of a cliché. It might invoke the pleasures of real coffee even in remote rural cafés, or three types of pure virgin olive oil on all supermarket shelves. But this is only one, rather utopian, interpretation of what is happening to the world. There are costs. One is this manipulation of the global in the interest of the powerful. For many in the world an appeal to patriotism or to another fundamentalism has become, as Lasch argues, 'the last refuge of the powerless, the vocabulary with which the disenfranchised give voice to their sense of betrayal'. Also resonant is the idea that globalization means global risk – oil spills, fall-out, ozone depletion and so on do not restrict themselves to national boundaries. Sociologist Ulrich Beck in his 1986 book *Risk Society* sees us moving into this stage from industrial society. The latter was characterized by the distribution of goods, and globalization by a distribution of 'bads', or dangers.

Globalization is both actual and perceptual, it is about how we live and what we fear. It is paradoxically both potentially enriching and dangerous. (We might like global warming because it means warmer Augusts for us in the UK even though we are persuaded that globally it is a bad thing.) It addresses 'who says' (authority) questions and 'who am I and where do I belong' (identity) questions.

The second feature of the end of the twentieth century is the development in the world of work of post-Fordism. When Henry Ford began his five-dollar, eight-hour day in his car-producing assembly lines his aim was to produce a standardized product, to ensure worker compliance with his production method and to give those workers enough take-home pay that they could take advantage of the consumer products, of all sorts, that were proliferating. This was a model of production and employment that prevailed for many years. Huge firms would employ large numbers of people who would each contribute a small part to the overall product. By the 1970s there was a falling demand for standardized, mass-produced goods and there was considerable competition for established manufacturing concerns from Pacific-rim countries. The response was to develop systems of flexible manufacturing – shifts from one product to another could be effected quickly; there was more concern with consumer wishes; there was the recognition that production could be dispersed – some places would just assemble components produced in a number of dispersed establishments.

New technologies proliferated, new patterns of management developed and global interconnections were pursued.

Two main impacts of this are crucial. First, job security goes. The idea of jobs for life, or of expecting to go into a firm and stay there for as long as one wishes, is no longer realistic. Even the semblance of paternalism is stripped from employers. One can either interpret this as exciting or scary. Without doubt the element of anxiety in many people's lives increases. The second impact is to separate the worker from any sense of the integrity of what is produced. Rock singer Bob Seger sang of the Detroit car-assembly line where his narrator was, in the song's title, 'Making Thunderbirds': 'They were long and low and sleek and fast and all you've ever heard. We were young and strong, we were making Thunderbirds'. There may be elements of macho nostalgia in this but there is also a lament for something lost that we should mourn losing.

Part of Ford's approach was to give workers enough to become consumers, and hence to consume motor cars, among other things. Alongside globalization and post-Fordist production we also have the development of a consumerist society. The individual is primarily a consumer not producer. Ford's rationale has been turned on its head – people are mobilized as consumers, their needs become more important than their labour power. Indeed it is consumption and consumers which define the symbolic shape of the society we live in. Shopping centres and TV commercials, not production lines and Thunderbirds, sit at the core of our society. But it is a core that is founded on the self-referential and the unreal. Baudrillard believes that the distinction between objects and their representations is dissolved. Rob Weatherill, in this book, has contributed to this debate. The quest for some division between the real and unreal is futile as the late twentieth century witnesses an unprecedented destruction of meaning. Language becomes the focus for attention, not the things it represents, people talk of leisure time and quality of life as something to be manufactured and slotted into their diaries, just like people talk about landscape after the assault on nature is well under way. It is an approach to life perhaps best undermined by the homily that it has never been heard that a person on their deathbed said, 'I wish I could have spent more time at the office.'

Postmodernism

The three areas of change identified above, globalization, post-Fordism and consumerism are often discussed as component parts of postmodernism. Indeed that such far-reaching changes are incorporated alerts us to the fact that postmodernism is something that seeks to address ideas, cultural experience and social conditions. It is an approach that, perhaps in the shadow of Auschwitz and the Gulags, argues meta-narratives (systems of thought that seek to answer from within their own frame of reference many or all dimensions of life – Marxism is an example) no longer have anything to offer, including the defining meta-narratives of the modern age that we, humanity, were making progress and that 'reason' and 'science' were the motor forces for this.

We are of course using terms in a particular way here. Modern is not used in the way you might find it defined in a dictionary as 'now or of the present'. Here it represents a particular historical period that began with the Enlightenment and was invigorated by the rise of democracies, by the industrial revolution, by scientific discoveries and technological innovation. Roberto Calasso in his book *The Ruin of Karsh* (1994) describes the modern as being 'born when the eyes observing the world discern in it this chaos, this monstrous confusion, but are not unduly alarmed. On the contrary, they are thrilled by the prospect of inventing some strategic move within the chaos, a new game ...' He uses the analogy of chess to describe an accelerating world where power struggles no longer take place on a chess board where one move follows the other with ceremonial slowness, but within a stream far stronger than everything it swept along ... a torrent. Perhaps the most telling metaphor for the modern is the one Karl Marx borrows from Shakespeare's *The Tempest* and uses in *The Communist Manifesto* to describe the tremendous energy of the bourgeois revolution with its factories and mass production. It is as if 'All that is solid melts into Air.'

This speed of change, characteristic of the modern, catches up everything in society. But it has caught up things and carried them along in its wake at different speeds. There remain historical strata laid down each on the other and the resulting milieu in which we live our lives has been much more nuanced than those grand theories of how our lives are determined would have us believe. It is in this recognition of the nuanced, and through it a critique of the shortcomings of the theory of modernity, and the realization that 'progress' has not brought the rewards it was assumed it would bring, that has contributed to the development of a postmodern perspective.

Postmodernism offers the approach of shifting the emphasis in the way we look at society from seeing an overall pattern to accepting diversity. For example, we speak not of history but histories. Difference and diversity replace categorization and order. Some postmodern voices are stark in their observations, Baudrillard sees melancholy as the norm in our meaningless societies. Arthur Kroker, author of the *Panic Encyclopedia* (1989), sees panic as the 'key psychological mood of postmodern culture ... marked by its *fin-de-millennium* swings from deep euphoria to deep despair'. Other commentators are complacent: Francis Fukuyama made a bestseller of his *The End of History* and is seeking to do the same with his follow up *Trust*. Liberal capitalism and closely knit cultures are, for him, the answer. So is it either meaninglessness and despair or complacent smugness?

But we should ask if all of this is being overstated. One danger seems to be that postmodernism becomes a new all-embracing theory – the king is dead, long live the king. Maybe we need to be able to sit with ambivalence and diversity and not seek to explain things away by 'reason' or answer anything with the cliché of postmodernism. An example of living with ambivalence and ambiguity can be found in Ulrich Beck's book of essays *Ecological Enlightment,* where he talks about science; it is like love, you can't live with it, but you can't live without it. In the future 'science is often enlightenment and anti-enlightenment, truth and concealment, liberation from inherited constraints and confinement in self-created objective constraints'.

The positives of living with ambivalence are one of the themes of this book, and have been explored in a number of our contributors' chapters, in particular those by Andrew Samuels and Bob Hinshelwood. In developing the case that a loss of certainty offers possibilities as well as challenge, our contributors are saying something not only about social change but also about psychoanalysis. Let's take the position of Freud to illustrate this point. Freud sought to ally himself with science and with the rational. But, in effect, although he may have wanted to be a man of his time he was also challenging many of the assumptions of it. In particular he challenged the assumption that as individuals we are masters of our own mental life. After Freud we have to accept that our psychic reality is dynamic, contradictory and made up of many parts.

So too is social action. All is not immediately obvious. It does not follow that we should be cynical about apparent altruism or that we should not condemn injustice. But we should be aware of the ambivalence inherent in our mental and our social life. Further, psychoanalysis, despite some attempts at 'scientific' evaluation, is validated through the individual trying out its insights in their own lives, risking being different. It is because of these aspects of his work that some have felt able to claim Freud for postmodernism (Barratt, 1993).[1]

The last big-picture approaches

If these four areas of change and challenge are coming together in last years of the millennium it is also apparent that the psychological changes consequent upon them and contributing to them are profound. Twenty years ago, or thereabouts, three American writers – all politically radical – were describing what they saw as the malaise of modern man and his society. Richard Sennett identified *The Fall of Public Man* and Christopher Lasch *The Culture of Narcissism,* while Alvin Toffler spoke of *Future Shock* and its impact on people's sense of security in their world. They did not agree each with the other, but from their different perspectives were identifying an agenda that reciprocally linked social change with psychic change. They occupied that last frontier of modernity in their big-picture approach and influenced agendas during the period up to the present.

Sennett's book, written in the early 1970s and published in 1977, contrasted the practices that derived from those conventions that regulated impersonal relations in public with the development, the triumph, of a concern with the inner life. A decline in politics and the public exercise of religion and a rise in psychoanalysis and psychology have generated a Western world where people are concerned with their single life-histories, where there is an obsession with persons at the expense of social relations. Politics degenerates into the struggle for self-realization not social change. The stranger becomes a threat and the modern city a hostile place to be endured, a place the individual has to defend themselves against.

Lasch, in books published in 1979 and 1984, identified a society in which we did not have much of a real self left. We did not grow into selfhood through the necessary painful awareness of the tension between our unlimited aspirations and our limited understanding. We thought we had limitless options without consequences, the freedom to choose everything at once. It was a form of narcissism in which we defined who we were through our purchases and through opinion polls, our options were shaped by the communication industry. We became commodities ourselves, living in a world where reality and fantasy converged and where our stance was to adjust, to survive. Looking backwards generates a debilitating nostalgia and forwards engenders a dread of the future and a concern with preparing defences against it. We develop a 'Minimal Self' as a route to psychic survival in troubled times.

Toffler's *Future Shock* was published in 1969. It offers a psychosociological account of how individuals cope in a society predicated on a notion of change rather than certainty and stability. Shattering stress and disorientation and a corresponding attempt to retreat, terrified, into whatever certainty is on offer is one scenario, the nightmare of fragmenting fundamentalisms. Like our other two American radicals, Toffler has good titles and his book *The Third Wave* (1980) prophesies a technological revolution of equal import to the first, the agricultural economy, and the second, the industrial with its mass production. The technological allows for the 'demassing' of the world: no mass production, no mass consumption, no mass media and so on.

Toffler, Sennett and Lasch were extrapolating from the present they lived in. The futurist Toffler was less concerned than the other two with identifying the ills of the present but with seeing the way that changes now would impact later. In the 1980s both the grand sweep and the 'future' went out of fashion. The contributors to this book are picking up the baton and once again running with the idea that psychoanalysis and psychotherapy have significant things to contribute to understanding the past, present and future and offering ways to respond to it.

A hundred years of crises

Have there been other times when there has been a prevailing sense of nihilism, a state where no belief or no truth commands assent? Looking back to the end of the last century we can see a time when there was a prevailing obsession with decay, decline and degeneration. Friedrich Nietzsche pointed to the Assassins' motto that 'nothing is true, everything is permitted' and had he lived would have seen these ideas enacted on the battlefields of the Somme and then later in Auschwitz, Dresden, the Burma railway and Hiroshima.

W. H. Auden in considering the Second World War in his 1947 poem *The Age of Anxiety* saw the historical process breaking down and 'necessity being associated with horror and freedom with boredom'. Everyone was reduced to the anxious status of a shady character or a displaced person. Even the most prudent become worshippers of chance. More recently we have had the anxiety of the bomb and the sense of the death of the moral legitimacy of governments for a generation of Americans in the wake of the Vietnam War and Watergate. We have had great depressions and disenchanted youth, we have had greed extolled as virtue and famine and disease decimating parts of the world.

Indeed we might agree with a character in Rohinton Mistry's

recent novel, *A Fine Balance,* about struggle and survival in India, that 'Where humans were concerned, the only emotion that made sense was wonder at their ability to endure, and sorrow for the hopelessness of it all.'

Knowing and anxiety

William Carlos Williams's poem 'The Orchestra', written after the Second World War and Hiroshima, includes the lines:

Man has survived hitherto because he was too ignorant
to know how to realize his wishes. Now that he can realize
them, he must either change them or perish.

Science and technology have influenced our ability to act on the world. Mass communications mean we can have access to information about the world more easily and quickly than in the past. Psychoanalysis and the therapeutic culture mean we have a sense that knowing ourselves is something both within our grasp and desirable. But all this potential for knowledge has not made us less anxious.

Examples of the relationship between knowledge and anxiety can be found in science and then contemporary childhood. In Dorothy Rowe's chapter she pointed to the need for our society to become more scientific in the sense of being more cautious about our knowledge. Other contributors have talked about psychoanalysis and psychology. But other aspects of science have not figured centrally in this book as contributors have chosen other areas to concentrate on.

Science has shaped and framed both our anxieties and our sense of new opportunities, the bomb and easy air travel, for example. While it has solved some problems it has not contributed to a problem free world. For example, it has contributed to the defeat of some diseases but it has not ended disease. New things turn up – the new plague of HIV, for example. Science has expanded our range of knowledge but not made the world more understandable. As we become more modern we feel more medieval, more the prisoners of the mystery of it all. This may explain the popularity of those books which seek to claim quantum theory or cosmology for the Tao or the Zen (Capra, 1976; Zukav, 1976).

If we feel more medieval we also realize that despite the omnipresence of science and technology they have not enriched our lives in terms of the metaphors we use or the literature we create. George Steiner has lamented the way that the manned landing on the moon prompted no great painting, poem or metaphor (*Guardian*, 6 August 1994). Alistair Cooke reporting at the time of the landing remarked that 'the astronauts continued to bob around on the Sea of Tranquillity while we floundered on the ocean of banality' (*Guardian*, 22 July 1969). Those of us who sat up all night to watch the landing and to wonder at the first steps might have felt affronted when historian A. J. P. Taylor described it as the biggest non-event of the century. Perhaps he was right!

There are some exceptions. Norman Mailer in *Fire on the Moon* tried to locate the landing in its own time and in the timelessness of myth. Simon Armitage's poem 'Zoom!' (1993) gives the impression of cosmology as energy in a way that would have been impossible to imagine before the space era. But these and other examples are few. One joke about the technological impact of the space race on our everyday lives suggested all we had got from those countless millions of dollars was non-stick frying pans. Culturally we may have fared equally badly.

When the prevailing mood is not neglectful it is fearful and anti-utopian. Consider the marvellous images of the planet Jupiter sent back to earth via the Hubble telescope: their main impact here was to encourage us to think of the apocalypse that would happen if a comet were to crash into us, like the comet Shumacher-Levy that had crashed into Jupiter. Consider our popular science fiction with its bleak future of a hostile cyberspace, or of urban sprawl and climactic destruction, or the triumph of machines and their hostility to everything human.[2]

We can use the example of children growing up in the 1990s to illustrate what is essentially a gap between the surface appearance of knowledge of life and an increase in the anxiety children have to live with. It may be that children appear to know more about the world they live in but their contact with that world is increasingly mediated by adults. One example is that street games have been replaced by either organized activity under the watchful eye of adults, or TV, video and computers, also, of course, designed, marketed and controlled by adults. (We have discussed this phenomenon in the commentary on Rob Weatherill's chapter in this book.)

Valerie Sinason, in her chapter and elsewhere in her writing, has examined anxiety, violence and secrecy as they interact in such a way as to do harm to children in our society. Many parents believe the world is much less safe. The real dangers they experience are augmented by urban myths like those in recent novels by, respectively, Ian McEwan and Martin Amis: the child who goes round the corner of the supermarket aisle while her father is at the check-out and is never seen again (in *The Child in Time*), or the boy who is raped in the lavatory of his local park as his mother waited impatiently outside (in *The Information*).

We act in ways that are consistent with our fears and our use of statistics is distorted by us to correlate with emotional rather than intellectual beliefs.[3]

The fears and anxieties we have for children are not only of the catastrophic and dramatic sort. We are generally concerned about the world they will grow up in and the opportunities they will have, will they get a job, and so on. Such fears are not new. But they now are experienced in a context in which we do not assume that the immediate future will be generally better than the present or the recent past. That is new.

Uncertain living together

In this chapter we have considered the social role of psychoanalysis and the factors underlying changes in society in the late-twentieth-century world. The relationship between social and psychological change has been examined and anxiety scrutinized. We have then used science and childhood as two examples to illustrate how knowledge and anxiety can grow, side by side. The chapter's theme is concerned with the impact of a loss of certainties and a consequent pervasive sense of ambiguities that have to be negotiated. In this it echoes the themes that have been developed through this book.

Also, like the book as a whole, it communicates the sense that there is challenge but also opportunity in change and that there is not a blueprint to follow to chart a way out of uncertainty. Both psychoanalysis, as developed by our contributors, and postmodernism allow for an end of certainties and the negotiation of new sorts of intimacy. Life, like society, is built up from the bottom rather than determined from on high, or dictated by the past. Along with this comes the possibilities of a new way of living together.

It is not that anything goes. On the contrary. Sociologist Zygmunt Bauman, in a book published in 1993 called *Postmodern Ethics*, argued that 'the frustration of certainty is morality's gain'. We have to live more in the moment – not adhering to the past or building castles in the air for the future, but negotiating sustainable, moral and reciprocal encounters in our relationships, our families, our workplaces and our communities.

From this comes a new sort of politics, also a subject developed by many of the contributors to this book. Philosopher Simone Weil, in her book *Gravity and Grace*, identified 'obedience to the force of gravity' as being the greatest sin. If society is unbalanced we must add weight to the lighter scale. Justice is a 'fugitive from the camp of conquerors'. George Steiner has spoken of the importance of what he calls 'ballast'. He means the weight of knowledge, of learning and of memory, that we carry round with us. When the wind is light we can sail easily before it but when the gale blows and the sea is heavy we need that inner ballast. But we don't sail alone, we also need that sense of security that Susie Orbach describes as growing in the soil of emotionally literate relationships.

In our personal and in our social and political lives we need to learn to live peacefully with diversity and adventurously with intimacy. Living together in the future could mean in our social lives adding weight to the lighter scale and in our personal lives recognizing the need for ballast as we steer our course through uncertain seas.

Notes

1. Writers from the Frankfurt School, discussed above, have developed a critique of the validity of psychoanalysis in terms of the ability of the person to act effectively in their own world.

2. There are many examples, such as William Gibson's cyberpunk novel *Neuromancer* (1984), or Neal Stephenson's *Snow Crash* (1992), about which Tom Hiney (*Observer*, 21 January 1996) said, 'As with most sci-fi it is less about the future than a fragmenting present-day America gripped by virulent media panic and millennial angst.'

3. This section draws on *One False Move,* a Policy Studies Institute research study on children's independent mobility. It is also informed by the feature writing of Linda Grant in the *Guardian* (1996) and Louise Chunn in the Observer (10 March 1996), for example.

References

Armitage, S. (1993), '*Zoom!*', in M. Hulse, D. Kennedy, & D. Morley, (eds.), *The New Poetry*, WHERE: Bloodaxe.

Auden, W. H. (1966), *In Memory of Sigmund Freud, Collected Shorter Poems, 1927–1957.* Faber and Faber

Barratt, B. B. (1993), *Psychoanalysis and the Postmodern Impulse*, The Johns Hopkins University Press

Capra, F. (1976), *The Tao of Physics*, Flamingo

Debord, G. (1967), *The Society of the Spectacle*, Where: Zone Books

Fromm, E. (1942), *The Fear of Freedom.* Routledge Kegan Paul
  – (1949), *Man for Himself*, Routledge Kegan Paul
  – (1970), *The Crisis of Psychoanalysis*, Penguin

Hearst, L. (1993), 'Our Historical and Cultural Cargo and its Vicissitudes in Group Analysis', *Group Analysis,* Vol. 26

Hinshelwood, R. D. (1995), 'Psychoanalysis in Britain: Points of Cultural Access', 1883–1918. *International Journal of Psychoanalysis*, 76, p. 135.

Kitwood, T. (1988), 'From Free Associations: A New Radicalization of Psychoanalysis', *History of the Human Sciences* Vol. 1, No. 2

Lasch, C. (1979), *The Culture of Narcissism*, New York: W. W. Norton & Co.
  – (1984), *The Minimal Self*, New York: W. W. Norton & Co.

Richards, B. (1989), *Images of Freud*, Methuen

Rieff, P. (1966), *The Triumph of the Therapeutic*, Penguin

Zukav, G. (1976), *The Dancing Wu Li Masters*, Fontana

Notes on the Editors

David Kennard is Director of the Tuke Centre for Psychotherapy and Counselling and Head of Clinical Psychology at The Retreat. His two previous books are *An Introduction to Therapeutic Communities* (1983) and *A Workbook of Group Analytic Interventions* (1993), co-authored with Jeff Roberts and David Winter. He is editor of the journal *Therapeutic Communities*.

Neil Small is a Senior Research Fellow at the Trent Palliative Care Centre and the University of Sheffield. He is the author of two books, *Politics and Planning in the National Health Service* (1989) and *AIDS, the Challenge: Understanding, Education and Care* (1993).

Notes on the Contributors

R. D. Hinshelwood is Clinical Director of the Cassel Hospital. He is a member of the British Psychoanalytic Society, Fellow of the Royal College of Psychiatrists, Honorary Professor in the Department of Human Relations, University of East London, and Chairperson of the Association of Therapeutic Communities. He was the founding editor of *International Journal of Therapeutic Communities* and *British Journal of Psychotherapy*, and is the author of *What Happens in Groups* (1987), *A Dictionary of Kleinian Thought* (1991) and *Clinical Klein* (1994).

Eric Miller was an anthropologist in India and Thailand and an internal consultant to companies in the USA and India before joining The Tavistock Institute in 1958. His main field is organizational research and consultancy, combining systemic and psychodynamic perspectives. He works internationally. He has authored numerous papers and six books, the most recent being *From Dependency to Autonomy: Studies in Organizational Change* (1993).

Susie Orbach is a psychotherapist and writer. In 1976 she co-founded the Women's Therapy Centre in London and in 1981 the Women's Therapy Institute in New York. She has written four books including *Fat is a Feminist Issue* (1978) and *What's Really Going on Here?* (1994). She has also co-authored three books with Luise Eichenbaum including *What Do Women Want?*

Barry Richards is Professor and Head of the Department of Human Relations at the University of East London, and Co-Director of the Centre for Consumer and Advertising Studies there. He has written *Images of Freud* (1989) and *Disciplines of Delight* (1994).

Dorothy Rowe worked as a teacher and child psychologist in Australia before coming to England in 1968. After completing her PhD from Sheffield University she was head of the Lincolnshire Department of Clinical Psychology from 1972 to 1986, since when she has devoted her time to writing, research and teaching. She is the author of ten books including *Depression: The Way Out of Your Prison* (1983), *Beyond Fear* (1987) and *Dorothy Rowe's Guide to Life* (1995).

Andrew Samuels is Professor of Analytical Psychology at the University of Essex, a Training Analyst of the Society of Analytical Psychology, London, where he is in private practice, and a Scientific Associate of the American Academy of Psychoanalysis. He is responsible for six books including *A Critical Dictionary of Jungian Analysis* (1986), *The Plural Psyche* (1989) and *The Political Psyche* (1994). In addition to writing, lecturing and clinical work, he functions as a consultant for several groupings.

Valerie Sinason is a Research Psychotherapist at St George's Hospital Medical School, Psychiatry of Disability Department, and a Consultant Child Psychotherapist at the Tavistock Clinic and Anna Freud Centre. She is training as an adult psychoanalyst and completing a PhD. A poet and writer, her books include *Mental Handicap and the Human Condition* (1992), *Treating Survivors of Satanist Abuse* (ed., 1993), *Nightshift,* (poems, 1995) and *Memory in Dispute* (1996).

Rob Weatherill has a background training in education and teaching, but has for many years been in private practice as a psychoanalytical psychotherapist in Dublin. He is also a teaching and a supervisory analyst. He is an executive member of the Irish Forum for Psychoanalytic Psychotherapy and the Irish Psychoanalytical Association, and a member of the editorial board of the *Journal of the Irish Forum for Psychoanalytic Psychotherapy*. He is the author of *Cultural Collapse* (1994).

Stuart Whiteley is a consultant psychotherapist in private practice and a consultant to organizations. He was formerly Medical Director of the Henderson Hospital. He is a Fellow of the Royal College of Psychiatrists, President of the Group Analytic Society (London) and executive editor of the journal *Group Analysis*. He was secretary of the International Association of Group Psychotherapy from 1989 to 1995 and a founding member and past Chairman of the Association of Therapeutic Communities. He is the co-author of *Dealing with Deviants* (1972) and *Group Approaches in Psychiatry* (1979).